Knitting
The Complete Guide

©2008 Jane Davis

Published by

kp **krause publications**
An Imprint of F+W Publications

700 East State Street • Iola, WI 54990-0001
715-445-2214 • 888-457-2873
www.krausebooks.com

Our toll-free number to place an order or obtain
a free catalog is (800) 258-0929.

The following registered trademark terms, products and companies appear in this
publication: Anacapa Fine Yarns, Brown Sheep's Lamb's Pride™, Jaeger™,
Knit One Crochet Too's Paint Box™, Koigu KPM, Kureon by Noro, Lion Brand Yarn®,
Lorna's Laces™, Louet Gems®, Mountain Colors Hand Painted Yarn™,
Purled Llama Yarn Company, Rowan Yarns®, and Yarn Council of America™.

Library of Congress Control Number: 2007942698

ISBN-13: 987-0-89689-591-1
ISBN-10: 0-89689-591-2

Designed by Katrina Newby
Edited by Toni Toomey

Printed in China

Acknowledgments

I have had a great time working on this book. It has been a lot of fun trying out new stitch ideas, and collecting them together with many of the classics that I've used for years. There have been several people who have helped me get this book together that I would like to thank.

All the people at Krause Publications have been a joy to work with, especially my editor, Toni Toomey. Thank you, Toni, for your deadlines, attention to detail, and understanding and patience with the book as it developed.

Thank you, Candy Wiza, for saying yes to this idea, and for being so supportive and understanding. Thank you also to all the people who helped to get this book out, especially Chris Redmond our technical editor, and Katrina Newby, who designed the cover and layout of the book.

Thank you very much to Lois Varga, owner of Anacapa Fine Yarns, in Ventura California. It helps so much to bounce ideas off of someone, and you always have such good ideas to make knitting easier and more understandable.

Finally, I'd like to thank my family, Rich, Jeff, Andrew, and Jonathan, for living with my yarn that's still everywhere.

Table of Contents

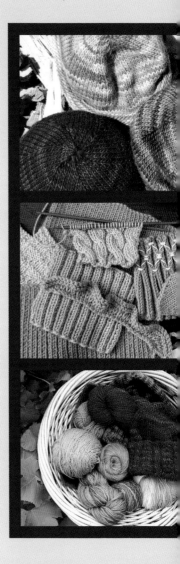

184 ~ Section 3 : Basic Projects

Introduction

I love books with collections of knitting patterns. There are so many now that you may ask why write another? Well, this book fills in some spaces left in other similar books. All of the charts (except the colorwork and embroidery sections) have both charts and line-by-line instructions, which is not found at one end or the other in most pattern libraries currently on the shelves. This book has a section on bead patterns in knitting, a subject close to my heart, and missing completely from most pattern libraries. Finally, in addition to two scarf patterns, this book has five basic patterns that I think are the staple for a knitter and make this a more complete basic reference than any other. These basics— a pair of mittens, a pair of socks, a hat, a dropped-sleeve sweater, and a set-in sleeve sweater—are great projects to use as a basis for future projects. Once you learn to make these projects to your size, you can use them to make many more projects of your own design, using swatch patterns from this or any other pattern book.

This book is meant for all levels of knitters, both as a how-to guide and as a reference. I hope you will come back to it again and again for ideas and as a ready source of information on all things knitting from classics to basic instructions. I have tried to put everything in this book that I would need as an ongoing reference. And I know I will be checking it often to look up a pattern or check techniques. So, this book I have written as much for myself as for you, so I will have all the information I need as a knitting reference that I haven't been able to find in one book.

—Jane Davis

Section 1: The Basics

From the types of yarn to choose and tools you will need, to how to knit and many of the techniques you will need for advanced knitting designs, here is your resource for learning to knit, and your reference to look up knitting techniques you want to try.

Yarn Fibers

Yarn is available in many fiber types, each with its own properties. The variety ranges from plant fibers, such as cotton, hemp, and linen, to animal fibers, such as wool, alpaca and angora, to synthetics. Many yarns are blends of several of these types of fibers, each lending an inherent characteristic that affects the feel and quality of the yarn. Following are descriptions of the fibers currently available.

Wool

Wool yarn, from any type of sheep, is the classic knitting yarn. It has a springy quality, making it ideal for most types of knitting. It gives a little as you knit, allowing you to accomplish many different types of stitches. The yarn can be course or soft, depending on many factors, including the type of sheep the wool comes from, the processing of the fibers, and the final treatment of the yarn.

Alpaca and Llama

Yarn made from alpaca is generally smoother and softer than wool yarn. Llama is somewhere in between the two. Both of these fibers have gained in popularity over the years as a softer alternative to wool yarn, though neither has as much of a springy quality as sheep's wool.

Mohair

Mohair yarn is characterized by long fibers that create a halo effect around a tightly twisted core yarn. Mohair yarn can be fine or thick and creates a fuzzy knitted fabric.

Silk

Silk yarn has a beautiful sheen in finished knitwear. Like cotton, it has very little give and can be a slippery yarn to work with, but the results are often worth the trouble. Yarn made from silk noil, or silk waste, has a matte texture, and similar properties to soft cotton.

Exotic Fibers

There are a growing number of exotic fibers on the market today, including angora from the angora rabbit, cashmere, yak, buffalo, quivit, and camel. These luxurious fibers, though expensive, produce very soft yarns, making them ideal for accents or small projects.

Cotton

Cotton yarn can be soft and fuzzy, or smooth with a soft sheen. Cotton yarn doesn't have as much spring as wool yarn, making it more difficult to work with though it is often preferred for cool summer knitting and making items that are not itchy.

Linen

Linen yarn is stiffer than cotton, but wears well when finished. It can go in the washer and dryer. It has a more fluid drape than cotton and softens with washings. Linen can be difficult to work with since it has no springiness.

Bamboo and Hemp

Bamboo yarn, like cotton, doesn't have as much spring as wool yarns, but it does have a lustrous sheen and softer drape than cotton or wool. It is easy to knit and comes in several weights. Hemp fiber is currently rougher than bamboo, with a natural unfinished look to the yarn.

Organic

To be truly organic the fibers must be grown and processed organically from start to finish. In the case of wool, this means for instance, that the sheep have been feed on organically grown grass, free of pesticides, and that the scouring of the wool was done with biodegradable cleaners. All spinning additives, such as oils, must be non-synthetic, and dyes must be non-metal, natural dyes. To be sure a fiber is truly organic, look for a certification on the label.

Synthetic

Acrylic, polyester, and other man-made fibers fall into this category. Yarns made from these fibers attempt to mimic natural fibers qualities or create new qualities of their very own. Because of the flexibility of this type of fiber, it can fit into almost all the qualities of the other fiber types, except that it is, of course not organic or natural.

Blends

Blends are any yarns made from a combination of two or more fibers. Most yarns today fall into this category, since blending fibers can create wonderful yarns that have all the good qualities of each different fiber, minimizing such things as the itchiness of wool, or the lack of spring in cotton.

Yarn Textures

When choosing yarn for your project, you can not only choose the type of fiber you want, but you can also choose from many yarn textures—from smooth, springy sock yarns, to airy, fluffy mohair blends, to sparkly metallic novelty yarns. Each type of yarn texture has it's own unique qualities that effect the knitting process and the look and feel of the project when it is finished. Following are descriptions of many of the types of yarn textures available today

Novelty Yarn

Novelty yarn is any yarn that has a texture that is unlike basic knitting yarns. This can mean any yarn from thin metallic knit-a-long yarns, to cords with long strands hanging from them.

Chenille

Chenille is a soft, fuzzy yarn that feels similar to velour fabric. It is made of a thin, tightly twisted core with short fibers radiating out perpendicular to the core, creating a round soft yarn. Most chenilles are made from synthetic, cotton, or silk fibers, and have similar properties to cotton. It can be difficult to knit with this type of yarn, as it tends to create uneven stitches. This can sometimes be corrected if you dampen the finished item and put it in the dryer. Be sure the try it with a large test swatch first though.

Eyelash

Eyelash yarn is characterized by long strands of fiber attached to a central core strand. Knit by itself, or held along with another type of yarn, eyelash yarn creates a soft airy, or furry effect, depending on the gauge of the knitting and the denseness of the long strands of fiber.

Home Spun

Yarns that give a home spun effect have thick and thin variations throughout the yarn. The variations from thick to thin can be minor or large, from very thick to very thin sections in the yarn. Home spun yarn is usually made from wool or wool-blend yarns.

Metallic

Metallic yarns can either have metal in them, or be made with a shiny material that looks like metal.

Mixes

Any of the yarn types in this section are often mixed together to create beautiful combinations of textures. A metallic or eyelash yarn is sometimes twisted with a plain yarn, such as homespun wool, to create a new texture and color. The yarn can be manufactured that way, or can be made from your own combinations that you hold together as one while knitting.

Railroad

This yarn is called by several names. It is characterized, by two thin parallel cords attached at regular intervals by a horizontal bar of threads that resemble railroad tracks or the rungs of a ladder. This yarn is flat like a ribbon and generally is less than ¼" wide. It is made of synthetic material.

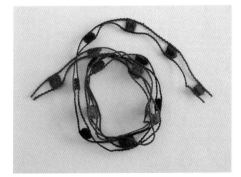

Ribbon and Tape

Ribbon comes in a variety of widths from less than ¼" to almost ¾", and is usually made from cotton, silk, wool blends, or synthetics. Tape yarn is a woven band of threads that is flat like ribbon, it can be as narrow as ⅛" wide up to ½" wide or more. You can make a ruffle with large loosely woven tape yarn by knitting into the side edge of the yarn with a thinner yarn, gathering the tape as you knit.

Roving

This is a hank of carded wool that has been drawn out into a long 1½" wide length ready to spin. It is soft and thick and easily pulls apart, so it takes some getting used to when knitting. To knit with it, you split it into thinner pieces and knit, overlapping new pieces as your get near the end of each section. *Pencil roving* is roving that has been split to about the size of a thick pencil and is ready to knit.

Spaced Accents

Spaced accents are thin novelty yarns with accents such as sequins or tufts of yarn spaced at regular intervals throughout a length of thread or thin cord. They are generally used by carrying them along with the main yarn so the strand of thread or cord is inconspicuous and the accents highlight the project.

Yarn Colors

Finally, after choosing a fiber and texture of the yarn for a project, there's the color. Some consider this the most important choice of all. The choices in yarn colors today are not just between different hues, but also between different methods of coloring, from machine-dyed solids to one-of-a-kind hand-painted skeins. You will need to choose how the color and process used to color your yarn will affect your finished project. Following are many of the choices of coloring currently available.

Machine-Dyed Solids

These yarns have solid, uniform colors throughout the skein. They usually have dye lot numbers on the labels so you can be sure that you have an exact color match in each skein. Don't fall prey to the temptation to slip in one skein from a different dye lot. It *will* show up in the knitted piece.

Hand-Dyed Solids

These yarns are solid colors, but because they are dyed in small lots by hand, the color of the yarn varies slightly throughout each skein, creating a subtle mottled effect in the finished knitwear. They sometimes have dye lot numbers and sometimes not, depending on the dyer's practices.

Hand Painted

Hand painted yarn is painted by hand by a dye artist. Each skein has it's own unique color sequence. Dye lots can be used for batches of the same colors used to dye a yarn, though each skein may have varying amounts of the different colors.

Machine-Dyed Variegated

In variegated yarn the color changes throughout the skein. The repeat is usually about one yard long. Machine-dyed variegated yarn has regular intervals of color changes. This is a good yarn for making projects where you want to align the colors throughout the knitting.

Space Dyed

Space-dyed yarn can be machine or hand dyed and refers to colors spaced throughout the skein. Machine-dyed variegated yarn is space dyed yarn, where the yarn might begin with a blue, then after about 6" it will change to purple, then magenta, then back to blue, and repeat the color sequence throughout the skein.

Spot Dyed

Spot dyed yarn is hand-dyed yarn where spots of color have been added to the yarn randomly, which may or may not show up through the entire skein in a regular repeat.

Progressive Colorations

This yarn falls into the variegated variety, however, the coloring of the yarn stays the same for several yards, then gradually changes to another color, and another, rarely repeating itself in one skein. When knitting with this yarn the project gradually changes from one color to the next throughout the knitting.

Tools and Terms
Knitting Needles

Straight needles are two pointed sticks with a ball at one end to keep the knitting from falling off. They can be wood, metal, plastic, or even glass. They can be basic and plain or made from exotic materials with decorative elements. Traditionally they come in 10" or 14" lengths, though there newer products that come in other lengths as well.

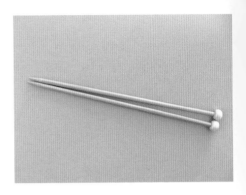

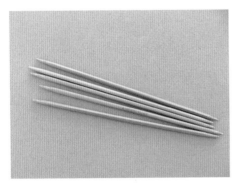

Double-pointed needles are for knitting in the round, creating a tube for small projects, such socks, or the body of a baby sweater. When knitting in the round on double-pointed needles the right side of the work always faces you, so you don't have to turn the work and purl on the wrong side. Double pointed needles usually come in sets of 4 or 5 needles, can range from 4" long to 14" long, and come in the same materials as straight needles.

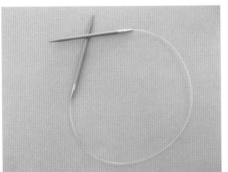

Circular needles are one long flexible cord with a 4" or 5" needle attached to each end. You can knit in the round or back and forth. Circular needles are available in different lengths ranging from 16" up to 32" long and come in the same materials as other needles.

Knitting needles come in variety of sizes. There are U.S. sizes and metric sizes that correspond to the diameter of the needle. Below is a chart of the U.S. sizes and the corresponding metric sizes.

Knitting Needles Sizes in U.S. and Metric

U.S.	Metric	U.S.	Metric	U.S.	Metric	U.S.	Metric
0	2	5	3.75	9	5.5	11	8
1	2.25	-	4	-	5.75	13	9
2	2.75	6	4.25	10	6	15	10
-	3	7	4.5	10½	6.5	17	12.7
3	3.25	8	5	-	7	19	15
4	3.5	-	5.25	-	7.5	35	19

Other Tools

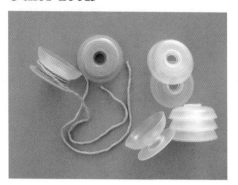

Bobbins are used for colorwork designs when only a small amount of yarn is needed. Short lengths of yarn are wound onto a bobbin that is used instead of having of the whole ball of yarn dangling from your work.

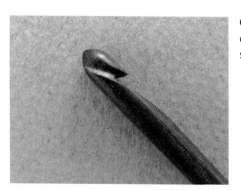

Crochet hooks are used in knitting for making crocheted edges and for picking up dropped stitches

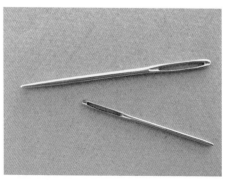

Tapestry needles are large blunt-ended needles used for weaving in the ends of yarn and seaming parts of a project together. Sewing needles can be used for adding beads to yarn or for sewing details onto the knitting.

A needle gauge has holes you slide your needles into to see what size the needle is. The smallest hole that your needle will slide into is the size of your needle.

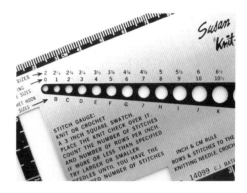

Point protectors are rubber tips that fit snugly on the ends of your needles to keep your work from sliding off when you're not knitting. They also keep your needles from poking into anything.

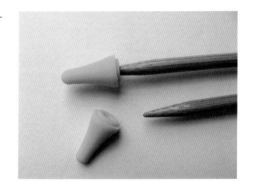

Row counters slide onto your needle and have dials that you can rotate to mark what row you are on in your knitting.

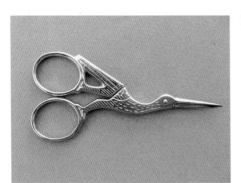

Scissors are a common tool used in knitting.

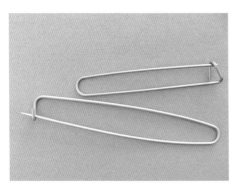

Stitch holders come in several shapes and sizes and are used to hold one or more stitches that you are not knitting at the moment, but will work with later. They can be used for anything from holding the stitches at a neckline while working the shoulders to cable knitting.

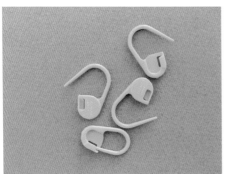

Stitch markers are small rings that slide onto the knitting needle between stitches to mark something you want to note, such as the beginning of the round in circular knitting, or a change in the pattern.

Straight pins and T-pins are used to hold your finished knitwear in place when you block your pieces to shape.

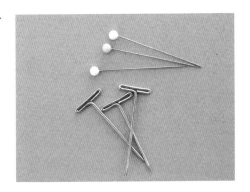

A tape measure is used throughout the knitting process to measure your gauge and your progress, and to help when blocking your finished piece.

Graph paper and pencils come in handy when altering the size or shape of a pattern, or when working on a design of your own.

Gauge

Gauge is a measurement of the number of stitches across 4" of knitting and the number of rows over 4" of knitting. It is the basis of pattern instructions for garment sizing and is critical in creating a project that matches the size indicated in the instructions. It is very important to knit a test swatch of your project with the yarn you will be using, then to measure and match the gauge indicated on the pattern. You can adjust your gauge by working in larger or smaller needles, changing the yarn you are using, or by changing the tension on the yarn as you knit.

Changing the way you wrap the yarn around your fingers can affect the gauge of your knitting, so it's important to get comfortable with a method and stick with it throughout a piece to help keep your knitting consistent throughout your work. You can hold the yarn loosely while knitting which creates a loose tension in the finished stitches, or you can wrap the yarn around one or more of your fingers to keep the yarn a little taunt to create more tension and tighter stitches. You will need to make a new test swatch for each new project, but it is well worth the extra time a text swatch takes in order to create a garment that matches the size you wish to make.

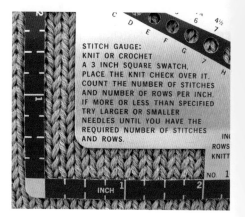

STITCH GAUGE:
KNIT OR CROCHET
A 3 INCH SQUARE SWATCH.
PLACE THE KNIT CHECK OVER IT.
COUNT THE NUMBER OF STITCHES
AND NUMBER OF ROWS PER INCH.
IF MORE OR LESS THAN SPECIFIED
TRY LARGER OR SMALLER
NEEDLES UNTIL YOU HAVE THE
REQUIRED NUMBER OF STITCHES
AND ROWS.

Tail and Working Yarn

When you cast on stitches to begin a row of knitting, you leave a *tail* of yarn that will be buried in the stitches when you finish off the piece. You then knit with the *working yarn*.

Abbreviations

Abbreviations are used in almost all knitting patterns to help make patterns take up less space. Following are the abbreviations that I have used for the instructions in this book. Most of them are standard terms used throughout the industry, with the exception of abbreviations used for knitting with beads. This have several variations, depending on which designer is writing the instructions.

*(asterisk) Repeat the instructions beginning at the asterisk the number of times indicated

**(double asterisks) repeat the instructions beginning at the double asterisks the number of times indicated

( ) (parenthesis) Same meaning as asterisks: Repeat the instructions inside the parentheses. Usually, the asterisks are used for lengthy instructions.

approx approximately

B(#) Knitting on the right side or purling on the wrong side, work the next number of stitches indicated by (#), sliding one bead into each stitch. This technique is used in plaited knitting, in which you knit into the back of the stitch on the right side and throw the yarn clockwise around the needle.

beg begin, begins, beginning

BO bind off

cir circular

cm centimeter (2.5 = 1 inch)

cn cable needle

CO cast on

cont continue

dec decrease, decreases, decreasing

dpn double pointed needle, double pointed needles

drp drop the yarn over from the previous row off the needle

foll following

ea each

g gram, grams

g st garter stitch

inc increase, increases, increasing

k knit

k2tog knit two stitches together as one

k3tog knit three stitches together as one

m1 make one

meas measure, measures

mm millimeter, millimeters

oz. ounce

p purl

patt pattern

pm place marker

psso pass slip stitch over

p2tog purl two stitches together as one

p3tog purl three stitches together as one

rem remain, remains, remaining

rep repeat, repeats

rnd(s) round, rounds

RS right side

SKP slip one, knit one, pass slipped stitch over knitted stitch

SK2P slip one, knit two together as one, pass slipped stitch over knitted stitches

s2kp slip two together as one, knit one, pass slipped stitches over knitted stitch

sld (#)B slide the number of beads indicated by (#) up to the needles to be caught between the stitch just finished and the stitch you will knit next

sl slip

st(s) stitch, stitches

St st stockinette stitch

tbl through back of loop

tog together

WS wrong side

wyib with yarn in back

wyif with yarn in front

yd.(s) yard, yards

yo yarn over

Yarn Weights and Skill Level Symbols

The Yarn Council of America has compiled the following chart of yarn weights and skill level symbols and descriptions to aid designers and knitters in displaying a clear understanding of the types of yarns used in projects and the skill levels expected to complete the projects. All projects in this book use the following symbols so you can quickly see if a project is suited to your yarn choice and skill level.

Yarn Weight Symbol and Category Names	1 SUPER FINE	2 FINE	3 LIGHT	4 MEDIUM	5 BULKY	6 SUPER BULKY
Types of Yarns in a Category	Sock, Fingering, Baby	Sport, Baby	DK, Light, Worsted	Worsted, Afghan, Aran	Chunky, Craft, Rug	Bulky, Roving
Knit Gauge Range in ST st to 4"	27 to 32 sts	23 to 26 sts	21 to 24 sts	16 to 20 sts	12 to 15 sts	6 to 11 sts
Metric Needle Size Range	2.25mm to 3.25mm	3.25mm to 3.75mm	3.75mm to 4.5mm	4.5mm to 5.5mm	5.5mm to 8mm	8mm and larger
U.S. Needle Size Range	#1 to #3	#3 to #5	#5 to #7	#7 to #9	#9 to #11	#11 and larger

BEGINNER

Projects for first-time knitters, using basic knit and purl stitches and minimal shaping.

EASY

Projects using basic stitches, repetitive stitch patterns, simple color changes, and simple shaping and finishing.

INTERMEDIATE

Projects with a variety of stitches, such as basic cables and lace, simple intarsia, double-pointed needles and knitting in the round needle techniques, plus mid-level shaping and finishing.

EXPERIENCED

Projects using advance techniques and stitches, such as short rows, fair isle, more intricate intarsia, cables, lace patterns, plus numerous color changes.

How to Knit

Knitting is very basic at the beginning, with many details and complexities revealing themselves as you learn more and more. This section starts out with the most basic cast on, describes how to knit one row and purl the next, and how to bind off. These steps are the first concepts that need to be understood and practiced so that you can progress to the many other possibilities knitting has to offer.

Following the elementary knitting steps, there are variations of casting on, progressing to increases, decreases, and all the specialty techniques beyond. Although the basic cast on shown in the first steps is easy to accomplish, it can be difficult to knit that first row. Just remember that most things are more difficult at the beginning and easier the more you practice. You will be knitting in no time!

Holding the Yarn: American and Continental

Traditionally, Americans have been taught to hold the working yarn in their right hand, while knitters in many European countries have been taught to hold the working yarn in their left hand. However, there is no right or wrong way to hold the yarn in knitting. Both ways of holding the yarn while knitting are effective.

In this book the illustrations and how-to instructions assume you are holding the working yarn in your right hand. As long as you can handle the yarn and needles and work the stitches, you are knitting. Whichever way you find the most comfortable and effective to hold the yarn and needles is the right way for you. For some stitches and techniques it may be easier to hold the yarn in one hand or the other (or both!), but other than that, it's your choice.

Making a Slip Knot

This is the first step in virtually all knitting projects. It is the process of creating an adjustable loop that you tighten onto your knitting needle.

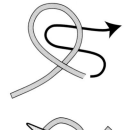

1. With the tail end of the yarn in your left hand, use your right hand to make a loop of yarn about 6" away from the end of the yarn.

2. Pass another loop of yarn up through the first loop from behind.

3. Slide the needle through the second loop. Pull the yarn ends to tighten the slip knot loosely on the needle. You want the slip knot to be the same size and tightness as your other cast on stitches.

Casting On: Simple Cast On

This is the easiest cast on, though it can be challenging to knit into the first row. You may prefer any of the other cast on techniques to this one, once you are comfortable with the more complex techniques. This cast on is still good to know how to accomplish, as it is used at various times in knitting, especially when knitting with beads along a beginning edge of knitting. Begin with a slip knot on the needle.

1. With the needle in your left hand, use your right hand to loop the working yarn and slide the loop onto the needle. It doesn't matter which direction you loop the yarn, just so you do it the same way each time.

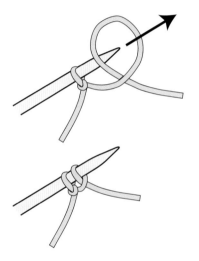

2. Tighten each loop loosely yet evenly on the needle before beginning the next loop.

Knit Stitch

This is the basic stitch in knitting that all other techniques begin with. You can make an easy scarf with just this stitch combined with a cast on and bind off.

1. Wrap the working yarn around one or more fingers of your right hand so there is a slight tension on the yarn and so the yarn is coming over your index finger about 1" away from the needle. Hold the needle filled with the cast-on stitches in your left hand and the empty needle in your right hand. With the working yarn to the back, *Slide the right-hand needle into the front of the first stitch on the left needle from left to right.

2. Loop the working yarn under the right needle counterclockwise. Think of the needle with the point, pointing at you, then wrap the yarn counterclockwise.

3. Pull the wrapped yarn through the loop on the left needle, sliding the old loop off the left needle and onto the right needle. You will have a new stitch on the right needle and one less stitch on the left needle. Repeat from asterisk for each loop on the left needle.

When you have knitted all the stitches off the left needle, move the stitch-filled needle to your left hand and the empty needle to your right hand, re-adjusting the yarn in your right hand, ready for the next row of knitting.

Purl Stitch

This is the other basic stitch in knitting. From this stitch and the knit stitch, all other stitches are created.

1. *With the working yarn to the front, insert the right needle into the front of the first stitch on the left needle from right to left.

2. Loop the yarn under and around the right needle counterclockwise.

3. Pull the new loop through the loop on the left needle, sliding the old loop off the needle. Repeat from asterisk for each loop on the left needle.

When you have purled all the stitches off the left needle, move the stitch filled needle to your left hand and the empty needle to your right hand, re-adjusting the yarn in your right hand, ready for the next row of knitting.

Bind Off

There are several techniques for binding off in knitting, but this one is the one most often used. You will need to work this process loosely, in order to keep this bound off edge the same tension as the rest of your knitting.

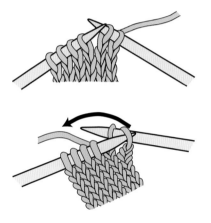

1. Knit the first two stitches.

2. Using the left needle, pick up the first stitch knitted on the right needle and pass it over the other stitch, and then slide it off the needle.

3. Knit another stitch and repeat step 2 for each pair of stitches on the right needle. When there is only one stitch remaining, cut the yarn to about 6" and pull the yarn through the final stitch.

Weave in Ends

Thread a tapestry needle with the yarn. Pass the needle through the wrong side of the knitting, following the path of the knitted stitches for about 2". Repeat in the opposite direction for added security. Trim the yarn leaving a ½" tail.

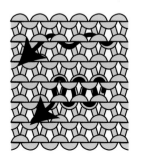

Knitting Details

All the following techniques build upon the basic steps for casting on, knitting, purling, and binding off. These techniques create wonderful textures, patterns, and color patterns that make knitting such a rich and beautiful form of expression.

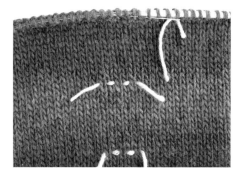

Casting On: Knitted Cast On

This cast on makes a thicker, more elastic edge that is much easier to knit into than the simple cast on described in the previous section

Make a slip knot and slide it onto the left needle. Using the right needle, knit one stitch into the slip knot, but rather than sliding the slip knot off of the left needle, leave it in place and slide the new stitch onto the left needle. Repeat, making each new stitch in the last stitch on the needle, until you have as many stitches as you need.

Casting On: Long-Tail Cast On

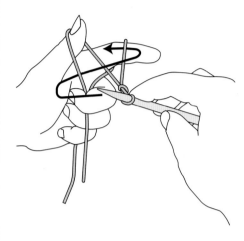

This is the cast on I use almost all the time. I like the rhythm used to make it, and it creates an even elastic edging to begin knitting from.

Beginning at a multiple of about 5" for every 10 stitches you need to cast on, make a slip knot, and slide it on to the right needle. Holding both the tail and working yarn in the last three fingers of your left hand, have the working yarn passing behind and over your index finger and the tail yarn coming from below and over your thumb as shown. *Keeping your tension tight, pass the needle under the yarn on your thumb and behind the yarn on your index finger. Let the yarn drop off of your thumb and use your thumb to tighten the new stitch on the needle. Repeat for each stitch. Move the stitch filled needle to your left hand to begin knitting.

Casting On: Provisional Cast On Using a Chain Stitch Base

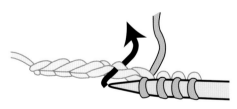

This is an easy cast on to use when you need to work off of the beginning row in the opposite direction.

With a crochet hook and a length of contrasting waste yarn, make a chain that has at least the same number of stitches as you need to cast on. Using a yarn that is thicker than your knitting yarn makes it easier to work the next step. Working through the loop of yarn on the back side of the chain, insert the knitting needle into one loop and pull the working yarn through, creating a stitch on the knitting needle. Repeat in enough loops on the chain so you have the desired number of stitches for your project. When you have finished knitting that section and want to work the stitches from the cast on row, simply pull out the chain stitches, while sliding the live stitches onto your needle.

Decreases: Knit Two Together

This decrease slants to the right and is the easiest and most common decrease in knitting.

Insert the right needle into the next two stitches on the left needle knitwise so that you are inserting the needle in the second and then the first stitch, as if they are one stitch. Finish knitting the stitch as usual. See illo for how needle enters from front to back.

Decreases: Knit Two Together Through the Back

This decrease causes the combined stitches to slant to the left. It is a common substitute for the slip, knit, pass over (SKP) technique.

Insert the right needle into the next two stitches on the left needle, purlwise on the back side of the stitch so that you are inserting the needle into the first stitch and then the second stitch as if they are one stitch. Finish knitting the stitch as usual.

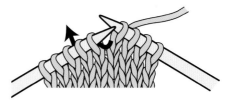

Decreases: Knit-Three-Together Centered Decrease

This decrease makes three stitches into one with the middle stitch centered over the two decreased stitches.

1. Insert the right needle into the next two stitches on the left needle, knitwise as one and slide them off the left needle and onto the right needle.

2. Knit the next stitch off the left needle.

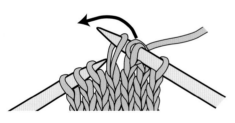

3. Pass the two slipped stitch over the knitted stitch and off the right needle. These stitches can be passed over the knitted stitch together in one motion, or one at a time.

4. The finished stitch will be centered over the two decreased stitches.

Decreases: Slip, Knit, Pass Over (SKP)

This is a common technique when you want your decrease stitches to slant to the left.

1. Insert the right needle into the first stitch on the left needle purlwise and slide it off of the needle.

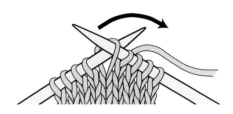

2. Knit the next stitch.

3. Pass the slipped stitch over the knitted stitch and off the right needle.

Increases: Yarn Over

This simple increase is the basis, along with decreases, of all lace work.

Wrap the yarn around the right needle once and then continue knitting. When you work the next row, knit or purl, as directed in the instructions, into the wrap as if it is a stitch. A small hole is created.

Increases: Knit into the Front and the Back

This is a quick and easy increase that creates a small texture where it is made, allowing you to easily find your increases when you need to work more on proceeding rows.

Knit into the front of the next stitch on the left needle, but don't slide the stitch off the needle yet. Instead, insert the right needle into the back of the knitted stitch purlwise and knit that loop, then slide it all off of the left needle. The result is two stitches on the right needle instead of one.

Increases: Knit into the Back of the Strand Below

This is a virtually invisible increase.

1. Using the right needle, lift up the strand between the stitches of the previous row.

2. Place it on the left needle, so that you can insert the right needle into the back of the stitch. Knit the stitch.

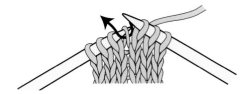

Assembling Pieces: Mattress Stitch

This stitch is used to join two pieces of knitting together in an almost invisible seam along the side edges. The trick is to pull the stitches tight enough to hold the two pieces together, but not so tight that you gather the fabric making it bunch up along the join.

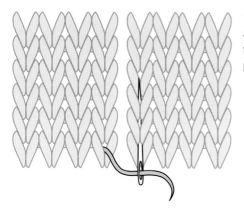

1. Thread the yarn with a tapestry needle and attach it to one edge of knitting half a stitch from the edge. Insert the needle in the other piece of knitting along the edge as shown.

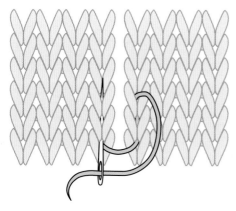

2. Insert the needle in the same location on the first piece that the yarn is exiting and make another stitch along the edge.

3. Repeat the last step on the edge of the other piece again.

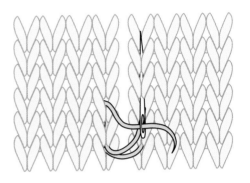

4. Pull the stitches, tightening them so that the two pieces of knitting come together and the stitches are hidden.

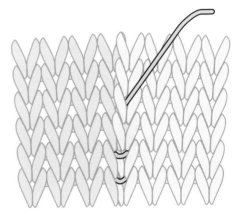

Assembling Pieces: Grafting or Kitchener Stitch

This stitch is used to join two edges of knitting together at the working ends using the live stitches of each piece and weaving a new row of knitting, joining the two pieces together at the same time. Sewing the seam with a tension that is the same as the knitted items is the key to getting the seam to look and feel the same as the knitted sections.

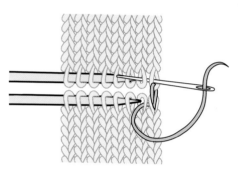

Cut the working end of one of the pieces of knitting to 3½ times the sections you need. Sew together and thread the yarn with a tapestry needle. Line the two pieces of knitting up as shown and pass the needle through the first stitch on the opposite piece then back through the first two stitches on the original piece. Always pass the needle down through the first stitch and up through the second stitch. Pass the needle through the first two stitches on the opposite piece as shown.

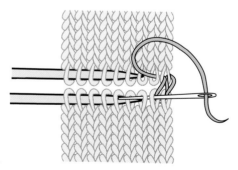

Repeat the process of passing the needle through two stitches on each side in the same manner, pulling the stitches you make so they are the same tension as the knitting, and slowly pulling the knitting needles out of the finished stitches as you work across the row.

Blocking

When you have finished knitting your project, before assembling it together, the finished pieces may not be the desired size or shape, or the stitches may be slightly uneven and the edges may tend to curl. Blocking is the process of adjusting the shape of your finished knitting so that it is the correct size and also evening out the stitches and edges so they are more uniform. Stitch patterns often dictate whether you will need to block your piece. Garter stitch for instance, is a very stable stitch that doesn't generally need blocking because it doesn't curl or slant. The amount that blocking can effect your knitting depends a great deal on the type of yarn used, the looseness of your pattern stitch and whether you are stretching the finished knitting a great deal in the blocking process. Generally animal and plant fibers tend to respond more to blocking than synthetics, though this is not always the case, so it is a good idea to test block any swatches you make before beginning your project.

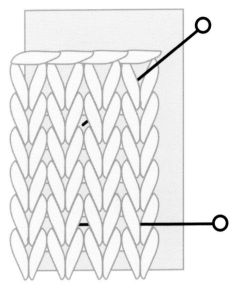

Dampen your knitting either by getting it wet and pressing out as much of the excess water as you can, or by steaming small pieces with a steam iron, or by rolling your knitting up in a damp towel to get it damp but not soaking wet. Lay your piece out on a flat surface and pin it to the finished measurements and let dry. Lace knitting is a special case, because to get the airy lace pattern you actually use quite a bit of strength to pull the fabric taunt to stretch it to it's finished size, while most other knitting is gently handled to pull it to it's finished size.

Short Rows

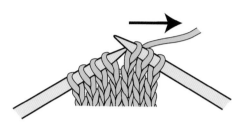

Short rows are when you are working flat, back and forth, and you turn your work in the middle of a row and knit in the opposite direction, before finishing knitting to the end of the row. You can just turn and work in the other direction but you will create a small hole in the knitting at the point where you change direction. There are several techniques to close the gap. One technique to keep a hole from forming, after you change direction, slip the first stitch before knitting in the new direction. In sock knitting this is the technique used for making the heel turn of the sock, though you are also decreasing stitches as you make the heel.

Picking Up Stitches Along an Edge

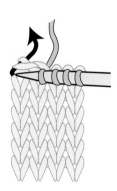

Picking up stitches along the edge of knitting is used when adding edgings to garments, and in many other projects such as when making a sock or knitting in entrelac. When picking up stitches along the side of a piece, you usually pick up 3 stitches for every 4 rows of knitting. When picking up stitches along a neckline, you usually need to pick up fewer stitches than correspond to the actual length along the opening so that the collar will not hang loosely.

Insert the needle into the edge of the knitting, wrap the working yarn around the needle and pull the yarn through, creating a stitch on the needle. Continue in this manner along the edge.

Embellishment Techniques

In addition to the wonderful knitting stitches you can use in knitting, you can also embellish your finished knitting with a variety of techniques, from felting to embroidery.

Cables: Right Cross Two over Two

Cables are wonderful design elements that add texture and interest to any design. There is a huge number of possible combinations of stitches. Here are the basic right and left cross techniques.

Pick up the next two stitches with the cable needle and hold the cable needle to the back of the knitting.

Knit the next two stitches on the left needle, then knit the two stitches from the cable needle. The four stitches will be crossed, two over two, with the front stitches slanting to the right.

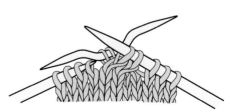

Cables: Left Cross Two Over Two

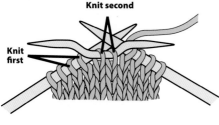

Knit second

Knit first

Pick up the next two stitches with the cable needle and hold the cable needle to the front of the knitting.

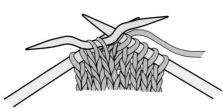

Knit the next two stitches on the left needle, then knit the two stitches from the cable needle. The four stitches will be crossed, two over two, with the front stitches slanting to the left.

I-Cord

This is a great little technique that has a lot of design possibilities. I-Cord is great for making straps on purses and bags, for braiding and for making three dimensional creations.

Using two double pointed needles, cast on 3 to 5 stitches. Knit across the stitches, then without turning to work in the other direction, slide the knitting to the other end of the needle, pull the working yarn around the back of the knitting and knit across the row again. Repeat this sliding and knitting step to create a small tube of knitting.

Bobbles

Bobbles are another big textural knitted element. They can be small or large depending on how many stitches you increase to make the bobble and how many rows of knitting you work onto the bobble stitches before decreasing back down to one stitch again.

Knit alternately into the front and the back of the stitch where you want to make the bobble from 3 to 5 or 6 times. Turn and purl across the new stitches. Turn and knit across the new stitches. Turn and purl across the new stitches.

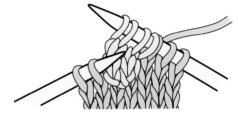

Now, decrease down to one stitch again by either knitting all the stitches together as one, or passing all of the stitches over the stitch closest to the end of the needle (you can do this one by one, not all at once).

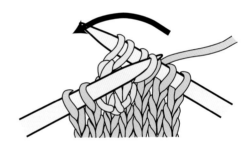

Making Buttonholes

Buttonholes can be as simple as a yarn over, which creates a small hole in the knitting so you can slide a small button through. To make larger buttonholes, you need to work the rows on one side of the buttonhole location for a few rows, then with a new length of yarn, work the same number of rows on the other side of the buttonhole. Finally you work across all the stitches, which creates the top of the buttonhole and joins the sections back together again. You can leave your finished buttonholes as is, or you can embroider around the openings with buttonhole stitch in the same yarn you used to knit your garment, or with a decorative yarn or thread.

Knitting Backwards

Knitting backwards comes in handy when you have a small section that needs to be worked and you don't want to turn your knitting around to purl that section of your project. Entrelac is one of the most common instances where knitting backwards is good to know.

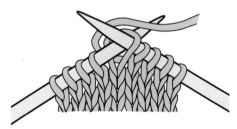

To knit backwards in stockinette stitch, hold the knitting and yarn as you would for working in knit stitch on the right side of the work. *Insert the left needle into the back of the first stitch on the right needle, wrap the yarn around the right needle counter clockwise, and slide the old stitch off the right needle. You will have one stitch knitted onto the left needle and one less stitch on the right needle. Repeat from the asterisk for each stitch.

Knitting With Beads

Adding beads to your knitting is a specialized technique, which, although needing extra preparation time and a few extra steps in the knitting process, can be very rewarding in the resulting added sparkle and texture in your project. You can simply sew a few beads in place on your finished knitting, or, if you want to add more beads than you care to embroider, you can follow the techniques below in which you string the beads onto the yarn and work them into your knitting as you knit.

There are several things to consider when preparing to work with beads in your knitting. You will need beads that have holes large enough to string onto the yarn. Usually a size 8 (about 1/8" across) works well with fingering to DK weight yarn, while size 5 or 6 beads (about 3/16" across) usually work well with DK to worsted weight yarn. The bead hole is the important part of the bead, since some larger beads have small holes, so it is always important to string a few beads onto the yarn to make sure they will fit.

To string the beads, tie a 12" strand of thread near the end of the yarn and use a beading needle threaded on the thread to string the beads then slide them onto the yarn. When sliding beads along the yarn, slide small sections of about 4" of beads at a time so you are not too abrasive on the yarn. The yarn should be a smooth, without large slubs that can block the beads. Also, some yarns that are loosely woven are not the best for knitting with beads since they can break easily from the abrasion of sliding the beads along the yarn.

If you are knitting a large section with a lot of beads, it is easier to handle the beads and yarn if you use a bowl that you can put the ball of yarn in and let the yarn with beads on it pile up loosely in the bowl. That way you can keep it all together and easily slide the beads up or down the yarn, as you need to move them.

To begin knitting with the beads, slide only the beads you will need for the row up near the knitting needles and slide the remaining beads about 2 to 4 feet down the yarn. After you complete each row, check your work to make sure there are no mistakes, then slide the number of beads needed for the next row up to the needle.

Knitting Beads Into the Stitches

Bead knitting is the process of sliding beads into the stitches as you knit, locking each bead into the knitted stitch so that it stays on the front of the fabric. The beads are pre-strung onto the yarn before knitting. The whole knitted surface can be covered in beads, or a relief pattern can be created by following a design chart and only sliding the beads in place where indicated.

When the whole surface is covered in beads you have the option of stringing all one color of bead, or pre-stringing a colorwork pattern from a chart. It is a great technique for making intricate designs, because once you have done the tedious work of stringing the colored bead pattern, you get to knit and watch the color pattern grow. Whether stringing beads to cover the whole surface of knitting or to create a relief pattern, you will need to help the beads stay in place on the front of the fabric.

This technique, also called *plaited knitting* was developed by Alice Korach, founding editor of *Bead & Button* magazine, to hold the beads in place. For this technique you need to string the number of beads you will need onto the yarn before beginning to knit. If you are using a lot of beads, it is a good idea to string a small piece of paper, about ¼" to ½" diameter depending on the knitting needle size, between rows so you can check that you've knitted all the beads in each row before moving on to the next row.

1. String the beads onto the yarn before beginning. On the knit side, every stitch is worked by inserting the needle into the back of the stitch and wrapping the yarn around the needle in a clockwise direction. Position the bead about half an inch from the needle and slide it into the stitch as you make the stitch, pushing it through before completing the stitch. You will need all of your fingers working to maneuver the bead through. Holding the yarn taunt and pushing the bead through with the pointer finger on your left hand usually makes the process easier.

2. On the purl side of the work, purl in the usual manner, inserting the needle into the stitch purlwise and wrapping the yarn counterclockwise around the needle. When you want to add a bead to a stitch, position the bead about half an inch from the needle and slide it into the stitch as you make it, pushing it through before completing the stitch. Hold the yarn taunt as you work, and use your left thumb to help push the bead through to the other side.

Knitting Beads Between Stitches

Beaded knitting is the process of sliding one or more beads between stitches as they are made. This is an easy technique to learn with many design possibilities. You can use just a few beads scattered to give your knitting sparkle, or you can cluster beads together sliding several beads between stitches which will increase the width of your knitting at that point depending on how many extra beads you add to the row. The size of the bead in relation to the yarn is another consideration since if you use smaller beads, you can slide more between the stitches that with larger beads.

Bead will be on back side of work

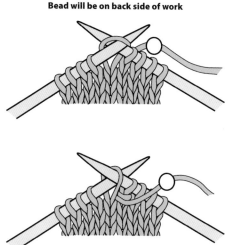

Bead will be on front side of work

String the beads onto the yarn before beginning. Work up to the place where you want the bead or beads, then slide the bead or beads up to the needle then work the next stitch. The bead will be on the purl side of the knitting when it has knit stitches on either side of it, and it will be on the knit side when has purl stitches on either side of it.

Here how to keep the beads on the right side of the fabric when knitting with the stockinette stitch: In a knit row bring the yarn to the front, purl one stitch, slide one bead up to stitch, purl one stitch, then bring the yarn to the back and continue knitting. On the purl side, bring the yarn to the back, knit one stitch, slide one bead up to the stitch, knit one stitch, then bring the yarn to the front and continue purling.

Colorwork

There are different methods of working color into your knitting. The color pattern determines which colorwork method is best to use.

Slip Stitch Method

Slipped stitches are used to make decreases. But slipping stitches can also be used in two-color knitted patterns. This method, also called masaic knitting, provides design possibilities that are almost unlimited. One noticeable characteristic of this colorwork method is the stitches that appear to be "stretched" vertically over two rows. These are the stitches that have been slipped in one row and then knitted two rows later, according to the pattern.

Every two rows are worked in one color, with the alternate rows worked in the second color. Stitches in each row are slipped and then knitted two rows later. Begin by casting on the number of stitches needed using one color of yarn. The knitting instructs will come with a chart with the color pattern. You will work with one color of yarn for two rows, first the knit row, then the purl row, slipping stitches as indicated by the pattern.

To slip a stitch on the knit row, insert the needle purlwise into the stitch and slide it off the left needle and onto the right needle. Continue knitting across the row to the next slipped stitch. If the pattern chart calls for you to slip more than one stitch, be sure to keep the working yarn tension loose and even across the back of the work. On the purl side of the work, purl the stitches indicated on the chart, and slip the indicated

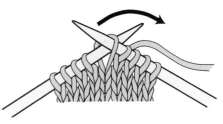

stitches purlwise. The working yarn will loosely strand across the slipped stitches as you work across the row. To begin the next knit row, drop the yarn color from the purl row, and pick up the color indicated on the right side of the chart. Then knit the row in the same manner as the first row.

To keep the yarn neatly twisted along the edge of your piece, always drop the old yarn and pick up the new yarn in the same manner every time you change yarns. For example, if you drop the old yarn in front and pick up the new yarn from behind the old yarn, the two yarns will neatly twist along the edge of the knitting.

Stranding Method

Stranded colorwork is the process of using two or more colors of yarn in a row of knitting.

Note: Some multicolored patterns in stranded knitting often appear to have a complex mix of colors in a single row. However, on closer look, you will see that, in most patterns, there are only two colors in a single row. In the stranding method, the color not in use is carried along the purl side, creating strands of yarn while the working color is being knitted. When the colors are switched, as dictated by the pattern, the stranded color becomes the working yarn, while the first color becomes the stranded yarn carried along the purl side.

One way to do stranded colorwork, is to hold the working yarn in one hand and drop the unused color until you need it. Another way to do stranded colorwork is to combine the American and Continental methods of holding the yarn. Hold the working yarn in your right hand, and the unused yarn in your left hand until it is needed. This makes it easier to keep the two yarns from twisting together as you switch colors. It also allows you to "weave" the unused yarn into the purl side of the knitting. Whichever way you hold the yarn, be careful to keep the tension on the stranded yarns very loose. If the strands are two tight, you will get puckers on the front side of the finished piece.

On the knit side of the work, hold the yarn to the back of the work, on the purl side, as shown, hold the yarn to the side facing you, using the color yarn for the pattern and stranding the unused yarn until needed.

Intarsia

Intarsia colorwork has solid blocks of color that make stranding impractical. The different colors of yarn are twisted at the color change so that they are linked together. Often times knitters will wind small amounts of yarn onto bobbins for small areas of color. Knit in the first color, then when changing to the second color, bring the new yarn up from under the old strand so that the two yarns are twisted together.

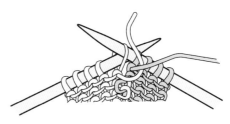

Felting

Felting, or fulling, is the process of taking an item made of wool and rubbing it in warm soapy water until it shrinks into a dense fuzzy fabric. Knitted bags are one of the best projects for this technique.

Crocheted Bind Off

Crochet edges are traditionally worked on knitted shawls, though you can use the technique on many projects. Instead of binding off at the end of your knitting, pick up 7 or 8 stitches with a crochet hook, *wrap the working yarn around the hook and pull through all the stitches. Work a row of about 12 chain stitches then pick up the next 7 or 8 stitches and repeat from the asterisk.

Swiss Darning

Also known as the duplicate stitch, this is the embroidery technique exclusive to knitting in which you add color to your finished knitting by stitching a contrasting colored yarn over the knitted stitches, following the path of the yarn.

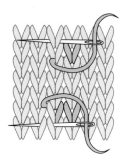

1. Work sideways, diagonally, or up and down, come up at the center of the base of the stitch to be covered.

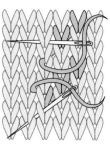

2. *Pass behind the next stitch above, insert the needle at the center of the base of the stitch where your first came up.

3. Exit at the center of the base of the next stitch to cover. Repeat from asterisk.

Elongated Swiss Darning

This variation of Swiss darning is worked the same as Swiss darning except that you carry each stitch over several rows of knitting, rather than just one stitch.

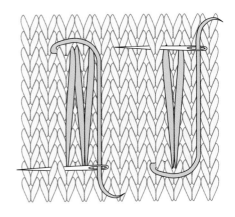

Straight Stitch

This is a very versatile stitch used for free-form embroidery and isolated stitches. If the stitches are more than an inch from each other it is a good idea to take a small stitch on the back side of the knitting so there won't be long loose strands. Come up from the back of the work where you want the stitch to begin and pass back down through the knitting where you want the stitch to end.

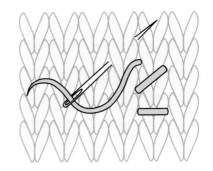

Back Stitch

This is strong stitch that is as good for seaming shoulder seams of garments as it is good for decorative stitching. Come up from the knitting one stitch length to the left of where you want the embroidery stitch, then back down one stitch length to the right. Come back up one stitch length to the left of where you began. You will have a long stitch on the back of the knitting and a short stitch on the front.

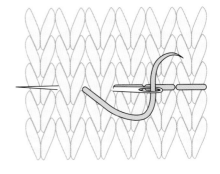

Stem Stitch

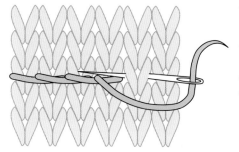

This is a great stitch for making stems of plants and outlining designs. Take a long stitch on the top of the knitting, then come back up about a one-half stitch length back and take another long stitch so each stitch overlaps the one before it.

Buttonhole or Blanket Stitch

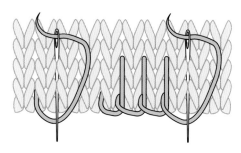

This traditional edging stitch can also be used as a decorative element. When the stitches are close together they form buttonhole stitch, and sewing them farther apart forms a blanket stitch. Begin with the yarn coming out on the left side of a knit stitch. Insert the needle one or two knit stitches away to the right, catching the yarn in the stitch as you pull the stitch into place.

Open Cretan Stitch

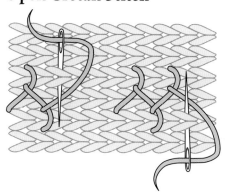

This easy decorative stitch is fun to work on knitting because the knitted stitches are like a grid helping you make the embroidered stitches even. Begin with the yarn coming out where the center of your embroidered row will be. Take a stitch toward the yarn, catching the yarn in the stitch as you pull through. Repeat the process in the opposite direction, counting the number of knitted stitches so that each cretan stitch is the same size.

Feather Stitch

This beautiful lacy stitch has many decorative uses. You can make a nice vine by continuing in one direction, then changing and working the other direction. With the yarn coming out on one side of a knitted stitch, take a diagonal stitch as shown, catching the yarn as you pull the stitch through. Take another stitch in the opposite direction. Continue alternating stitch directions. At the end of the row tack the last loop down with a small stitch.

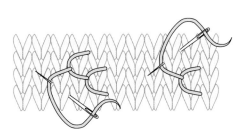

Chain Stitch

The chain stitch makes a bold line that adds a lot of color to your embroidery. Making a single loop and tacking it down is called lazy daisy stitch. Come up from the knitting where you want the chain to begin. Insert the needle in the same place and take a small stitch, looping the yarn around so that you catch the yarn in the stitch as you pull through. Repeat for each stitch. At the end of the row take a small stitch in the last loop to hold it in place.

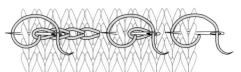

French Knot

French knots can be like tiny bobbles that decorate your knitwear. Be sure to pierce the knitting yarn so your knot doesn't slip to the back of the work. Come up from the back of the knitting where you want your knot to be. Wrap the yarn loosely around the needle three times. Holding the wrapped yarn insert the needle into the knitted fabric next to where the yarn is coming out, but not in the same hole. Carefully pull the yarn through creating a knot from the wrapped yarn.

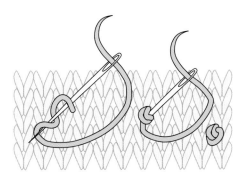

Smocking

Smocking on knitting is another interesting embellishment that adds a unique decorative touch to your finished project. To prepare for smocking, you will usually need to gather the finished knitting before working the smocking embroidery. You can smock without pre-gathering, but the finished piece is not as uniform and has a different look than the pre-gathered smocking.

1. To gather the knitting, use a thick pearl cotton, or other strong cord that is as long as the width of the knitting plus about 6". Thread a tapestry needle and make a large knot at the tail end. The knot needs to be large enough so it won't slip through the knitting.

2. Working along one row of knitting about three or four rows from the top edge, pass behind the first stitch. *Skip the next three stitches and pass behind the next stitch. Repeat from the asterisk across the knitting, unthreading the needle and leaving the end loose at the end. Repeat every 4 rows along the section to be smocked, then gather the knitting by pulling the ends of the threads until the knitting is snuggly gathered together. Tie each pair of threads into a knot to hold the gathering in place.

3. The smocking stitches can be worked in the same yarn used for knitting or in a contrasting yarn or decorative thread. The smocking stitches are made only in the column of knitted stitches that you passed behind when gathering the knitting. After completing your smocking stitches, cut and pull out the gathering stitches. The finished piece will loosen a little after you remove the gathering stitches.

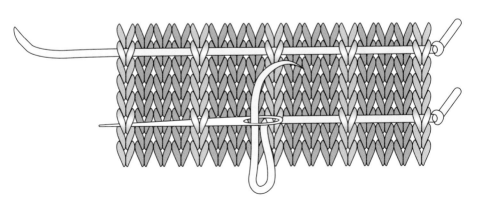

Smocking: Stem

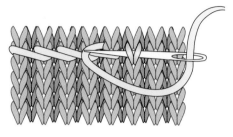

This is the same stitch as in the embroidery section above, except that you are working over several rows of knitting, pulling the knitting together into a smocked pattern as you go. Attach the yarn to the back of the knitting and come up on the left side of the first stitch to pleat. *Take a horizontal stitch behind the top of the next pleat or four stitches away and pull the two pleats together. Repeat from the asterisk for each stitch, keeping the yarn always on above the stitches.

Smocking: Cable

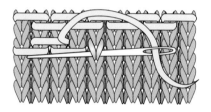

1. Make a single stem stitch by working from left to right, inserting the needle from right to left behind one pleat, with the yarn above the needle.

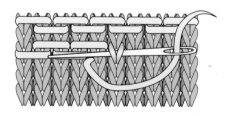

2. Make another stem stitch in the same manner as above, with the yarn below the needle. Pull the stitches to form a pleat Alternate these two stitches across the row.

Smocking: Van Dyke

1. Working from right to left, take a stitch through two pleats, then take another stitch through both pleats.

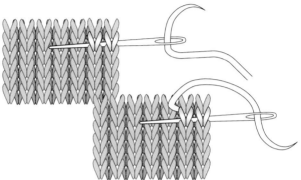

2. Take a stitch through the second and third pleats about 3 rows below. Take another stitch through both pleats. Repeat these two steps working up 3 rows, then down 3 rows.

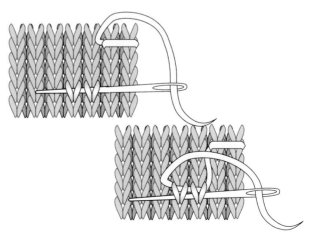

Smocking: Diamond

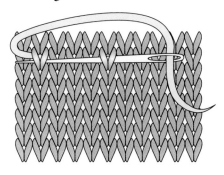

1. Beginning with the yarn coming out of the left side of the first stitch, pass the needle from right to left, behind the fourth stitch to the right and the beginning stitch.

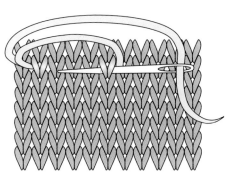

2. Take another stitch behind the rightmost knitted stitch. Pull the previous stitch tight, then finish pulling the current stitch to gather the knitted fabric.

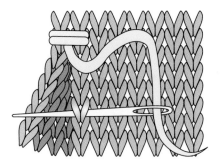

3. Pass the needle from right to left behind the stitch 4 rows below.

4. Pass the needle from right to left behind the fourth stitch to the right and behind the same stitch as the last step.

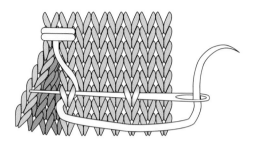

5. Pass behind the rightmost knitted stitch again and pull the stitches tight as in the first gathering.

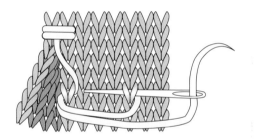

6. Pass the needle from right to left behind the stitch 4 stitches above.

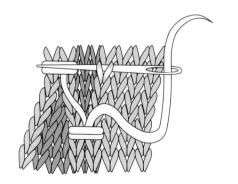

7. Pass behind the fourth stitch to the right and the stitch to the left.

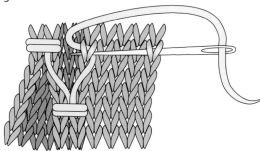

8. Pass behind the rightmost stitch again and tighten the stitches, gathering the knitted fabric. Continue in this manner across the knitting.

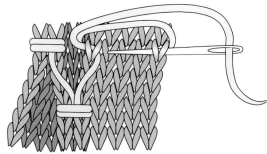

Using Charts

There are three basic types of knitting charts in this book—standard charts, slip-stitch charts, and colorwork charts. Each box represents one stitch and each row of boxes represents one row of knitting. The slip-stitch charts show you what color to cast on, while the other two types of charts assume you have already cast on your stitches before beginning the chart. The coloring in standard charts denotes right-side and wrong-side rows. Slip-stitch and colorwork charts use the color to indicate the different colored yarns.

Standard Knitting Charts

The standard knitting charts use common symbols to indicate the different types of stitches, shown in the diagram below. The charts are numbered for working flat with the knit side rows numbered on the right and the purl side rows numbered on the left. The knit side rows are white and the purl side rows are tinted pale blue or gray.

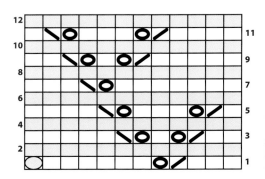

Chart Symbols

Chart symbols are the language of knitting in chart form. Many of the chart symbols I have used are standard symbols used throughout the industry. Some are my own adaptations to explain a step such as purling, then sliding a bead into place, then purling again.

☐	K on the right side, p on the wrong side
⊟	P on the right side, k on the wrong side
◺	SKP
◿	K2tog
🐾	Knit into the back of the stitch
◉	Yarn over
▲	K3og, centered decrease
◫	Slip one stitch
⊷①⊶	On the right side, p1, sld 1 bead, p1. On the wrong side, k1, sld 1 bead, k1
④	Make a 4 st bobble
⟩✕⟨	Move 2 sts to cn in front, k 2 sts, k sts from cn
⟩✕⟨	Move 2 sts to cn in back, k 2 sts, k sts from cn

Slip Stitch Charts

The slip stitch charts begin with a bar across the bottom. This shows the color yarn to use for casting on. The boxes on the right side of the chart show which color is used to knit that row. The patterns are worked in stockinette stitch. Each box represents one stitch and two rows of knitting. The vertical lines in the boxes mean that you slip that stitch when you come to it in the knitting, holding the working yarn behind the work on the knit row, and in front of the work on the purl row. Each row of the chart is numbered at both the right and the left side of the chart. That is because, other than the cast on row, each row of the chart is worked twice, once from right to left on the knit side of the work, and then once from left to right on the purl side of the work. After the final row of the chart, bind off in either color of yarn.

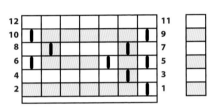 

Stranded Colorwork Charts

Each box represents one stitch and each row of boxes represents one row of knitting. The charts are numbered for working flat in stockinette stitch with the knit side rows numbered on the right and the purl side rows numbered on the left. However the charts can also be worked in the round by beginning each round at the right side of the chart and following the pattern to the left.

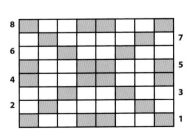 

Tips for Success

The following tips and techniques are not necessary steps for completing a project, but they do help make knitting projects go more smoothly and quickly, or help to give your project a more carefully finished look.

- After finishing a difficult section of a pattern, use a contrasting yarn to thread through the stitches on the needle, so that if you need to undo your knitting to correct something later on, you will be able to keep the finished work through your current section. This is a great technique for lacework, since it is sometimes difficult to pick up all the stitches in a row when you rip back.

- Use a sticky note to mark your place in your pattern, covering the rows you haven't worked yet.

- Selvedges are sometimes included in a garments instructions, but usually not. You may want to cast on an extra stitch at the beginning and end of the cast on and knit these on each row. These will be your selvage stitches that are sewn into the seam when you are through.

- Hems are sometimes helpful in knitted garments to keep the edge from rolling up, or to add weight to the finished item. An easy way to add a hem is to knit about an inch in stockinette stitch before beginning the stitch pattern, then purl one row, then begin your pattern. When you have finished your garment, you can fold up your hem at the purl row and sew it in place on the wrong side of the garment.

- When the instructions say to increase at both ends of a row, such as when making the sleeve of a sweater, make one increase at the end of the row before and the next increase at the end of the indicated row so that you will have neater edges of knitting.

- When making a garment for yourself, check the measurements against a similar item of your own that you like the fit and adjust the pattern to fit those measurements, such as lengthening or shortening the sleeve or body.

- When casting on, be careful to make your cast on stitches, even, yet not too tight. If you find that your cast on stitches are tighter than the rest of your knitting, you can use a larger sized needle for your cast on row, or hold two needles together as one while casting on, then remove the extra needle after the first row.

- To make sure that your sewn in tails stay put, try to pass back over the same tail thread, piercing it so it stays in place.

Section 2: Stitch Patterns

Stitch patterns are what make knitting an ever interesting and exciting endeavor. There are classics, that have been with us for many generations, and new designs that bring something different to our projects. Just the simple change of one part of a pattern can create a whole new look to a design. Following are patterns old and new, easy and challenging, some with texture and some with color, and each with it's own look and characteristic.

Knit and Purl Patterns
1 Garter Stitch

This pattern is reversible.
Begin with any number of stitches.
Row 1: Knit.
Row 2: Knit.
Repeat rows 1 and 2 to continue the pattern.

2 Stockinette

Begin with any number of stitches.
Row 1: Knit.
Row 2: Purl.
Repeat rows 1 and 2 to continue the pattern

3 Reverse Stockinette

Begin with any number of stitches.
Row 1: Purl.
Row 2: Knit.
Repeat rows 1 and 2 to continue the pattern.

4 Plaited

Begin with any number of stitches.
Row 1: K in the back of ea st.
Row 2: Purl.
Repeat rows 1 and 2 to continue the pattern.

5 Seed

This pattern is reversible.
Begin with a multiple of 2 stitches.
Row 1: (K1, p1) rep across.
Row 2: (P1, k1) rep across.
Repeat rows 1 and 2 to continue the pattern.

6 Moss

This pattern is reversible.
Skews toward the right before blocking.
Begin with a multiple of 2 stitches.
Row 1: (K1, p1) rep across.
Row 2: (K1, p1) rep across.
Row 3: (P1, k1) rep across.
Row 4: (P1, k1) rep across.
Repeat rows 1–4 to continue the pattern.

7 Broken Garter Stitch

This pattern is reversible.
Begin with a multiple of 2 stitches.
Row 1: (K1, p1) rep across.
Row 2 and 3: K.
Repeat rows 1–3 to continue the pattern.

8 Checker

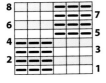

Begin with a multiple of 6 stitches.
Row 1–4: (K3, p3) rep across.
Row 5–8: (P3, k3) rep across.
Repeat rows 1–8 to continue the pattern.

9 Checker Stripe

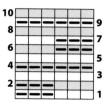

Begin with a multiple of 6 stitches.
Row 1 and 2: (K3, p3) rep across.
Row 3: Knit.
Row 4: Knit.
Row 5: Knit.
Row 6: (P3, k3) rep across.
Row 7: (P3, k3) rep across.
Row 8: Purl.
Row 9: Purl.
Row 10: Purl.
Repeat rows 1–10 to continue the pattern.

10 Dotted Diagonals

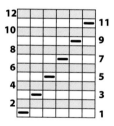

Begin with a multiple of 6 stitches.
Row 1: (K5, p1) rep across.
Row 2 and all even rows: Purl.
Row 3: K4, p1, (k5, p1) rep to last st, k1.
Row 5: K3, p1, (k5, p1) rep to last 2 sts, k2.
Row 7: K2, p1, (k5, p1) rep to last 3 sts, k3.
Row 9: K1, p1, (k5, p1) rep to last 4 sts, k4.
Row 11: (P1, k5) rep across.
Repeat rows 1–12 to continue the pattern.

11 Dotted ZigZag

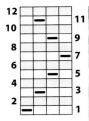

Begin with a multiple of 4 stitches.

Row 1: (K3, p1) rep across.

Row 2 and all even rows: Purl.

Row 3 and 11: K2, (p1, k3) rep across, ending with k1 instead of k3.

Row 5 and 9: K1, (p1, k3) rep across, ending with k2 instead of k3.

Row 7: (P1, k3) rep across.

Repeat rows 1–7 to continue the pattern.

12 Mountain Ridges

Begin with a multiple of 12 stitches.

Row 1: (P1, k2, p1, k4, p1, k2, p1) rep across.

Row 2: P1, k1, (p2, k1) rep to the last st, p1.

Row 3: ((K2, p1) twice, (p1, k2) twice) rep across.

Row 4: (K1, p2, k1, p4, k1, p2, k1) rep across.

Row 5: K1, p1, (k2, p1) rep to the last st, k1.

Row 6: ((P2, k1) twice, (k1, p2) twice) rep across.

Repeat rows 1–6 to continue the pattern.

13 Mountain Stripes

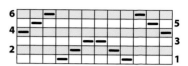

Begin with a multiple of 12 stitches.

Row 1: K3, (p1, k4, p1, k6) rep across, ending with k3 instead of k6.

Row 2: P4, (k1, p2, k1, p8) rep across, ending with p4 instead of p8.

Row 3: K5, (p2, k10) rep across, ending with k5 instead of k10.

Row 4: K1, (p10, k2) rep across, ending with p1 instead of p2.

Row 5: K1, (p1, k8, p1, k2) rep across, ending with k1 instead of k2.

Row 6: P2, (k1, p6, k1, p4) rep across, ending with p2 instead of p4.

Repeat rows 1–6 to continue the pattern.

14 Stacked Mountains

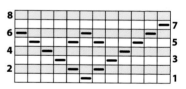

Begin with a multiple of 12 stitches.

Row 1: K6, (p1, k11) rep across, ending with k5 instead of k11.

Row 2: P4, (k1, p1, k1, p9) rep across, ending with p5 instead of p9.

Row 3: K4, (p1, k3, p1, k7) rep across, ending with k3 instead of k7.

Row 4: P2, (k1, p5, k1, p5) rep across, ending with p3 instead of p5.

Row 5: K2, (p1, k2, p1, k1, p1, k2, p1, k3) rep across, ending with k1 instead of k3.

Row 6: (K1, p4, k1, p4, k1, p1) rep across.

Row 7: (P1, k11) rep across.

Row 8 P.

Repeat rows 1–8 to continue the pattern.

15 Steps

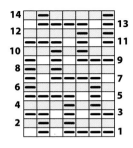

Begin with a multiple of 7 stitches.
Row 1: (P4, k1, p1, k1) rep across.
Row 2: ((P1, k1) twice, p3) rep across.
Row 3: (P2, k1, p1, k1, p2) rep across.
Row 4: (P3, (k1, p1) twice) rep across.
Row 5: (K1, p1, k1, p4) rep across.
Row 6: (K1, p4, k1, p1) rep across.
Row 7: (K1, p4, k1, p1) rep across.
Row 8: (K1, p1, k1, p4) rep across.
Row 9: ((P3, (k1, p1) twice) rep across.
Row 10: (P2, k1, p1, k1, p2) rep across.
Row 11: ((p1, k1) twice, p3) rep across.
Row 12: (P4, k1, p1, k1) rep across.
Row 13: (P1, k1, p4, k1) rep across.
Row 14: (P1, k1, p4, k1) rep across.
Repeat rows 1–14 to continue the pattern.

16 Stripes and Pillars

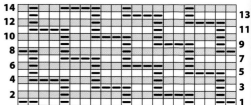

Begin with a multiple of 21 stitches.

Row 1: P2, (k2, (p1, k5) twice, p1, k2, p4) rep across, ending with p2 instead of p4.
Row 2: P4, (k1, p5, k1, p2, k4, p2, k1, p5) rep across, ending with p1 instead of p5.
Row 3: K1, (P1, k5, p1, k2, p4, k2, p1, k5) rep across, ending with k4 instead of k5.
Row 4: P1, (k4, p2, (k1, p5) twice, k1, p2) rep across, ending with p1 instead of p2.
Row 5: K1, (p4, k2, (p1, k5) twice, p1, k2) rep across, ending with k1 instead of k2.
Row 6: P1, (k1, p5, k1, p2, k4, p2, k1, p5) rep across, ending with p4 instead of p5.
Row 7: K4, (p1, k5, p1, k2, p4, k2, p1, k5) rep across, ending with k1 instead of k5.
Row 8: K2, (p2, (k1, p5) twice, k1, p2, k4) rep across, ending with k2 instead of k4.
Row 9: K1, (p1, k2, p4, k2, p1, k5, p1, k5) rep across, ending with k4 instead of k5.
Row 10: P4, (k1, p2, k4, p2, k1, p5, k1, p5) rep across, ending with p1 instead of p5.
Row 11: K1, ((p1, k5) twice, p1, k2, p4, k2) rep across, ending with, k1 instead of k2.
Row 12: P1, ((k1, p5) twice, k1, p2, k4, p2) rep across, ending with p1 instead of p2.
Row 13: K4, (p1, k2, p4, k2, p1, k5, p1 k5) rep across, ending with k1 instead of k5.
Row 14: P1, (k1, p2, k4, p2, k1, p5, k1, p5) rep across, ending with p4 instead of p5.
Repeat rows 1–14 to continue the pattern.

17 Triangle Wedges

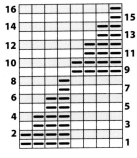

Begin with a multiple of 8 stitches.

Row 1 and 2: (K4, p4) rep across.

Row 3: K4, (p3, k5) rep across, ending with k1 instead of k5.

Row 4: P1, (k3, p5) rep across, ending with p4 instead of p5.

Row 5: K4, (p2, k6) rep across, ending with k2 instead of k6.

Row 6: P2, (k2, p6) rep across, ending with p4 instead of p6.

Row 7: K4, (p1, k7) rep across, ending with k3 instead of k7.

Row 8: P3, (k1, p7) rep across, ending with p4 instead of p7.

Row 9 and 10: (P4, k4) rep across.

Row 11: (P3, k5) rep across.

Row 12: (P5, k3) rep across.

Row 13: (P2, k6) rep across.

Row 14: (P6, k2) rep across.

Row 15: (P1, k7) rep across.

Row 16: (P7, k1) rep across.

Repeat rows 1–16 to continue the pattern.

18 Reversible Triangles

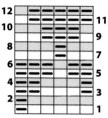

Begin with a multiple of 6 stitches.

This pattern is reversible.

Row 1: (K5, p1) rep across.
Row 2: (K1, p5) rep across.
Row 3: P1, (k3, p3) rep to last 5 sts, k3, p2.
Row 4: K2, (p3, k3) rep to last 4 sts, p3, k1.
Row 5: P2 (k1, p5) rep to last 4 sts, k1, p3.
Row 6: K3, p1, (k5, p1) rep to last 2 sts, k2.
Row 7: K2, (p1, k5) rep to last 4 sts, p1, k3.
Row 8: P3, k1, (p5, k1) rep to last 2 sts, p2.
Row 9: K1, (p3, k3) rep to last 5 sts, p3, k2.
Row 10: P2, (k3, p3) rep to last 4 sts, k3, p1.
Row 11: (P5, k1) rep across.
Row 12: (P1, k5) rep across.
Repeat rows 1–12 to continue the pattern.

19 Dotted Diamonds

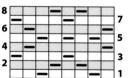

Begin with a multiple of 8 stitches.
Row 1: K1, (p1, k3, p1, k3) rep to last 7 sts, p1, k3, p1, k2.
Row 2: P3, (k1, p1, k1, p5) rep to last 5 sts, k1, p1, k1, p2.
Row 3: (K3, p1) rep across.
Row 4: (P1, k1, p5, k1) rep across.
Row 5: K1, p1, (k1, p1, k3) rep to last 7 sts, (p1, k1) rep 3 times, k1.
Row 6: (P1, k1, p5, k1) rep across.
Row 7: (K3, p1) rep across.
Row 8: P3, (k1, p1, k1, p5) rep to last 5 sts, k1, p1, k1, p2.
Repeat rows 1–8 to continue the pattern.

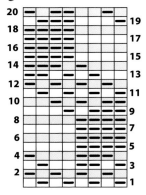

20 Tumbling Blocks

Begin with a multiple of 8 stitches.
This pattern is reversible.
Row 1: (P1, k1) rep across.
Row 2: (K1, p1) rep across.
Row 3: (P1, k1, p2, k2, p1, k1) rep across.
Row 4: (K1, p3, k3, p1) rep across.
Row 5–8: (P4, k4) rep across.
Row 9: (P3, k1, p1, k3) rep across.
Row 10: (P2, k1, p1, k1, p1, k2) rep across.
Row 11: (P1, k1) rep across.
Row 12: (K1, p1) rep across.
Row 13: (K2, p1, k1, p1, k1, p2) rep across.
Row 14: (K3, p1, k1, p3) rep across.
Row 15–18: (K4, p4) rep across.
Row 19: (P1, k3, p3, k1) rep across.
Row 20: (K1, p1, k2, p2, k1, p1) rep across
Repeat rows 1–20 to continue the pattern.

21 Mini Tumbling Blocks

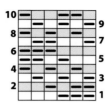

This pattern is reversible.

Begin with a multiple of 6 stitches.

Row 1: (P3, k3) rep across.

Row 2: (P2, k1, p1, k2) rep across.

Row 3: (P1, k1) rep across.

Row 4: (K1, p1) rep across.

Row 5: (K1, p1, k1, p2) rep across.

Row 6: (K3, p3) rep across.

Row 7: (P1, k2, p2, k1) rep across.

Row 8: (K1, p1) rep across.

Row 9: (P1, k1) rep across.

Row 10: (K1, p2, k2, p1) rep across.

Repeat rows 1–10 to continue the pattern.

22 Large and Small Diamonds

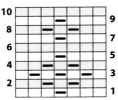

Begin with a multiple of 7 stitches.

Row 1, 5, 7 and 9: K3, (p1, k6) rep across, ending with k3 instead of k6.

Row 2, 4 and 8: P2, (k1, p1, k1, p4) rep across, ending with p2 instead of p4.

Row 3: ((K1, p1) rep 3 times, k2) rep across, ending with k1 instead of k2.

Row 6 and 10: P.

Repeat rows 1–10 to continue the pattern.

23 Diamond Stripes

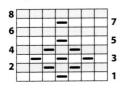

Begin with a multiple of 7 stitches.

Row 1, 5 and 7: K3, (p1, k6) rep across, ending with k3 instead of k6.

Row 2 and 4: P2, (k1, p1, k1, p4) rep across, ending with p2 instead of p4.

Row 3: (K1, p1) rep three times, k1) rep across.

Row 6 and 8: P.

Repeat rows 1–8 to continue the pattern.

24 Leaf Rows

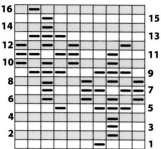

Begin with a multiple of 10 stitches.
Row 1: K3, (p1, k9) rep across, ending with k6 instead of k9.
Row 2 and 4: P7, (k1, p9) rep across, ending with p2 instead of p9.
Row 3: K2, (p1, k9) rep across, ending with k7 instead of k9.
Row 5: K1, (p3, k2, p1, k4) rep across, ending with k3 instead of k4.
Row 6: (P2, k1, p2, (k1, p1) twice, k1) rep across.
Row 7: (P2, k1, p2, k2, p1, k2) rep across.
Row 8: (P2, k1, p2, (k1, p1) twice, k1) rep across.
Row 9: K1, (p3, k2) rep across, ending with k1 instead of k2.
Row 10: ((K1, p1) twice, (k1, p2) twice) rep across.
Row 11: (K2, p1, K2, p2, k1, p2) rep across.
Row 12: ((K1, p1) twice, k1, p3, k1, p1) rep across.
Row 13: K6, (p3, k7) rep across, ending with k1 instead of k7.
Row 14: P2, (k1, p9) rep across, ending with p7 instead of p9.
Row 15: K7, (p1, k9) rep across, ending with k2 instead of k9.
Row 16: P1, (k1, p9) rep across, ending with p8 instead of p9.
Repeat rows 1–16 to continue the pattern.

25 Fir Tree

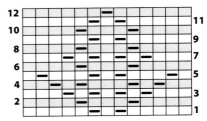

Motif has 11 stitches.
Row 1, 9 and 11: K4, p1, k1, p1, k4.
Row 2, 6, 8 and 10: P3, k1, p3, k1, p3.
Row 3 and 7: K2, (p1, k1) rep 4 times, k2.
Row 4: P1, k1, p1, k1, p3, k1, p1, k1, p1.
Row 5: P1, k3, (p1, k1) twice, k2, p1.
Row 12: P5, k1, p5.

26 Garter Heart

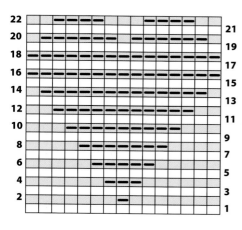

Motif has 15 stitches.
Row 1 and all odd rows: Knit.
Row 2: P7, k1, p7
Row 4: P6, k3, p6.
Row 6: P5, k5, p5.
Row 8: P4, k7, p4.
Row 10: P3, k9, p3.
Row 12: P2, k11, p2.
Row 14: P1, k13, p1.
Row 16 and 18: Knit.
Row 20: P1, k6, p1, k6, p1.
Row 22: P2, k4, p3, k4, p2.

27 Garter Spiral

Begin with a multiple of 21 stitches.

Row 1 and all odd rows: Knit.

Row 2: P6, k8, p7.

Row 4: P4, k12, p5.

Row 6: P2, k5, p7, k4, p3.

Row 8: P1, k4, p3, k5, p3, k3, p2.

Row 10: K4, p2, k9, p2, k3, p1.

Row 12: K3, p2, k3, p6, k2, p2, k3.

Row 14: K3, p2, k3, p2, k2, p2, k2, p2, k3.

Row 16: P1, k2, p2, k3, p2, k5, p2, k3, p1.

Row 18: P2, k2, p2, k3, p7, k3, p2.

Row 20: P8, k9, p4.

Row 22: P10, k5, p6.

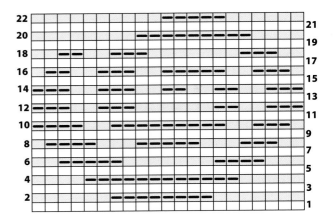

Ribbing Patterns
28 Classic K1 P1

Begin with a multiple of 2 stitches, plus 1.
Row 1: (P1, k1) rep to last st, p1.
Row 2: K1, (p1, k1) rep across.
Repeat rows 1 and 2 to continue the pattern.

29 Classic K2 P2

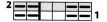

Begin with a multiple of 4 stitches, plus 2.
Row 1: (P2, k2) rep to last two sts, p2.
Row 2: K2, (p2, k2) rep across.
Repeat rows 1 and 2 to continue the pattern.

30 Uneven Stripes

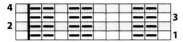

Begin with a multiple of 11 stitches, plus 1.
Row 1: K1, (p2, k3, p2, k1, p2, k1) rep across.
Row 2: P1, (k2, p1, k2, p3, k2, p1) rep across.
Repeat rows 1 and 2 to continue the pattern.

31 Uneven Stripes Reversed

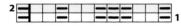

Begin with a multiple of 11 stitches, plus 1.
Row 1: P1, (k2, P3, k2, p1, k2, p2) rep across, ending
    with p1 instead of p2.
Row 2: K1, (p2, k1, p2, k3, p2, k2) rep across, ending
    with k1 instead of k2.
Repeat rows 1 and 2 to continue the pattern.

32 Reversible Dotted Rib

Begin with a multiple of 6 stitches, plus 3.
Row 1: (P3, k3) rep to last three sts, p3.
Row 2 and 4: K3, (p3, k3) rep across.
Row 3 (P1, k1) rep to last st, p1.
Repeat rows 1–4 to continue the pattern.

33 Checkered

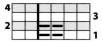

Begin with a multiple of 4 stitches, plus 2.
Row 1: (K2, p2) rep to last two sts, k2.
Row 2: (P2, k2) rep to last two sts, p2.
Row 3: K.
Row 4: P.
Repeat rows 1–4 to continue the pattern.

34 Garter Ridges

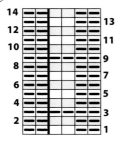

Begin with a multiple of 4 stitches, plus 2.
Row 1 and all odd rows except 3 and 9: (P2, k2) rep to
    last two sts, p2.
Row 2 and all even rows: K2, (p2, k2) rep across.
Row 3 and 9: K.
Repeat rows 4–9 to continue the pattern.

35 Brioche

Begin with a multiple of 2 stitches, plus 2.
Row 1: K.
Row 2: (K1, k in st below) rep to last two sts, k2.
Rep row 2 to desired length.

36 Garter Edged Rib

Begin with a multiple of 4 stitches, plus 2.
Row 1–4: K.
Row 5: K2, (p2, k2) rep across.
Row 6: P2, (k2, p2) rep across.
Rep row 5 and 6 to desired length.

37 Rolled Edge Rib

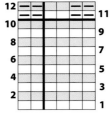

Begin with a multiple of 4 stitches, plus 2.
Row 1–10: Work in St st.
Row 11: P2, (k2, p2) rep across.
Row 12: K2, (p2, k2) rep across.
Rep row 11 and 12 to desired length.

38 Scalloped Edge Rib

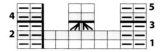

Begin with a multiple of 8 stitches, plus 2.
Row 1: P2, (k6, p2) rep across.
Row 2: K2, (p6, k2) rep across.
Row 3: P2, (k3togib, k3tog, p2) rep across.
Row 4: K2, (p2, k2) rep across.
Row 5: P2, (k2, p2) rep across.
Rep row 4 and 5 to desired length.

39 Bobble Edge Rib

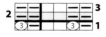

Begin with a multiple of 4 stitches, plus 2.
To make bobble: k1 into front, back and front of the
next st, making 3 sts from one. Working only in the
3 new sts, turn, p across 3 sts, turn, k across 3 sts,
turn, p across 3 sts, turn, k3tog.
Row 1: P1, MB, (k2, p1, MB) rep across.
Row 2: K2, (p2, k2) rep across.
Row 3: P2, (k2, p2) rep across.
Rep row 2 and 3 to desired length.

40 Crochet Loop Edge

Begin with a multiple of 4 stitches, plus 2.
Row 1: (K1, p2, k1) rep across.
Row 2: (P1, k2, p1) rep across.
Rep row 1 and 2 to desired length.
With crochet hook, *pick up 4 sts, yo, pull through all
    sts on hk, ch 7, rep from asterisk for all sts.

41 Cable Edge

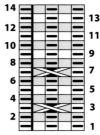

Begin with a multiple of 4 stitches, plus 1.
Row 1, 5, 9, 11, and 13: (P1, k1) rep to the last st, p1.
Row 2, and all even rows: K1, (p1, k1) rep across.
Row 3 and 7: (P1, LC1x2) rep to the last st, p1.
Repeat rows 12 and 13 to desired length.

42 Cable and Rib

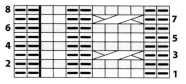

Begin with a multiple of 10 stitches, plus 2.

Row 1: (P2, k4, p2, k2) rep to the last 2 sts, p2.

Row 2, and all even rows: K2, (p2, k2, p4, k2) rep across.

Row 3 and 7: (P2, RC2x2, p2, k2) rep to the last 2 sts, p2.

Repeat rows 1–3 to desired length.

43 Cable and Garter Ridge

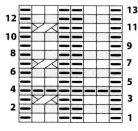

Begin with a multiple of 8 stitches.

Row 1, 5, 9 and 13: P1, (k2, p2) rep across, ending with p1 instead of p2.

Row 2, and all even rows, except row 4: K1, (p2, k2) rep across, ending with k1, instead of k2.

Row 3, 7, and 11: P1, (k2, p2, RC1x1, P2) rep across, ending with p1, instead of p2.

Row 4: K.

Repeat rows 4–13 to desired length.

44 ZigZag

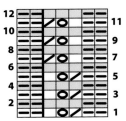

Begin with a multiple of 10 stitches, plus 2.
Row 1: (K2, p2, 1 over 1 cross, k2, p2) rep to last two
sts, k2.
Row 2 and 4: (P2, k2, p4, k2) rep to last 2 sts, p2.
Row 3: (K2 p2, k2, 1 over 1 cross, p2) rep to last two
sts, k2.
Repeat rows 1–4 to desired length.

45 Rib Triangle

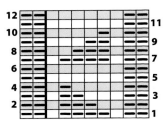

Multiple of 8 stitches, plus 2
Row 1: (P2, k1, p4, k1) rep to last 2 sts, p2.
Row 2: (K2, p1, k3, p2) rep to last 2 sts, k2.
Row 3: (P2, k3, p2, k1) rep to last 2 sts, p2.
Row 4: (K2, p1, k1, p4) rep to last 2 sts, k2.
Row 5 and 11: (P2, k6) rep to last 2 sts, p2.
Row 6 and 12: (K2, p6) rep to last 2 sts, k2.
Row 7: (P2, k1, p4, k1) rep to last 2 sts, p2.
Row 8: (K2, p2, k3, p1) rep to last 2 sts, k2.
Row 9: (P2, k1, p2, k3) rep to last 2 sts, p2.
Row 10: (K2, p4, k1, p1) rep to last 2 sts, k2.
Rep rows 1–12 to desired length.

46 Eyelet

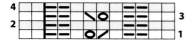

Begin with a multiple of 10 stitches, plus 2.

Row 1: (K2, p2, k1, k2tog, yo, k1, p2) rep to last two sts, k2.

Row 2 and 4: (P2, k2, p4, k2) rep to last 2 sts, p2.

Row 3: (K2 p2, k1, yo, SKP, k1, p2) rep to last two sts, k2.

Repeat rows 1–4 to desired length.

47 Eyelet Columns

Begin with a multiple of 12 stitches, plus 2.

Row 1: (K2, p2, k1, yo, SKP, k2tog, yo, k1, p2) rep to last 2 sts, k2.

Row 2, and all even rows: P2, (k2, p6, k2, p2) rep across.

Repeat rows 1 and 2 to desired length.

48 Eyelet ZigZag

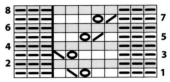

Begin with a multiple of 8 stitches, plus 3.
Row 1: (P3, k2, yo, SKP, k1) rep to last 3 sts, p3.
Row 2 and all even rows: K3, (p5, k3) rep across.
Row 3: (P3, k3, yo, SKP) rep to last 3 sts, p3.
Row 5: (P3, k1, k2tog, yo, k2) rep to last 3 sts, p3.
Row 7: (P3, k2tog, yo, k3) rep to last 3 sts, p3.
Repeat rows 1–8 to desired length.

49 Wave

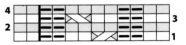

Begin with a multiple of 5 stitches, plus 2.
Row 1, 3 and 5: (P2, k2tog, yo, k1) rep to last 2 sts, p2.
Row 2 and all even rows: K2, (p3, k2) rep across.
Row 7, 9 and 11: (P2, k1, yo, k2tog) rep to last 2 sts, p2.

50 Lace Stripes Rib

Begin with a multiple of 8 stitches, plus 2.

Row 1: (P2, k1, yo, SKP, k2tog, yo, k1) rep to last 2 sts, p2.

Row 2 and all even rows: (K2, p2) rep to last 2 sts, k2.

Repeat rows 1 and 2 to desired length.

51 Leaves

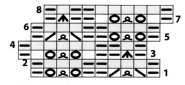

Begin with a multiple of 10 stitches.

Row 1: P1, (SKP, k1ib, k2tog, p2, yo, k1ib, yo, p2) rep across, ending with p1 instead of p2.

Row 2 and 6: K1, (p3, k2) rep across, ending with k1 instead of k2.

Row 3: P1, (k3tog, p2, k1, yo, k1ib, yo, k1, p2) rep across, ending with p1 instead of p2.

Row 4: K1, (p5, k2, p1, k2) rep across, ending with k1 instead of k2.

Row 5: P1, (yo, k1ib, yo, p2, SKP, k1ib, k2tog, p2) rep across, ending with p1 instead of p2.

Row 7: P2, (k1, yo, k1ib, yo, k1, p2, k3tog, p2) rep across, ending with p1 instead of p2.

Row 8: P1, (k1, p2, k5, p2) rep across, ending with p1 instead of p2.

Repeat rows 1–8 to desired length.

Cables
52 Two Over Two Left Cross

Begin with 4 stitches (bordered by reverse stockinette).

Row 1: K.

Row 2 and all even rows: P.

Row 3: LC2x2.

Repeat rows 1–4 to continue the pattern.

53 Two Over Two Long Left Cross

Begin with 4 stitches (bordered by reverse stockinette).

Row 1, 5 and 7: K.

Row 2 and all even rows: P.

Row 3: LC2x2.

Repeat rows 1–8 to continue the pattern.

54 Three Over Three Left Cross

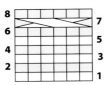

Begin with 6 stitches (bordered by reverse stocki-
nette).
Row 1, 3 and 5: K.
Row 2 and all even rows: P.
Row 7: LC3x3.
Repeat rows 1–8 to continue the pattern.

55 Two Over Two Alternating

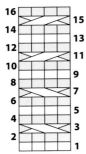

Begin with 4 stitches (bordered by reverse stocki-
nette).
Row 1, 5, 9 and 13: K.
Row 2 and all even rows: P.
Row 3 and 7: LC2x2.
Row 11 and 15: RC2x2.
Repeat rows 1–16 to continue the pattern.

56 Keyhole

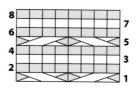

Begin with 8 stitches (bordered by reverse stockinette).
Row 1 and 5: K.
Row 2 and all even rows: P.
Row 3: RC2x2, LC2x2.
Row 7: LC2x2, RC2x2.
Repeat rows 1–8 to continue the pattern.

57 Mini Keyhole

Begin with 4 stitches (bordered by reverse stockinette)
Row 1 and 5: K.
Row 2 and all even rows: P.
Row 3: RC1x1, LC1x1.
Row 7: LC1x1, RC1x1.
Repeat rows 1–8 to continue the pattern.

58 Double Horseshoe

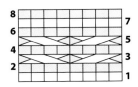

Begin with 8 stitches (bordered by reverse stockinette).
Row 1 and 7: K.
Row 2 and all even rows: P.
Row 3 and 5: RC2x2, LC2x2.
Repeat rows 1–8 to continue the pattern.

59 Braid

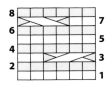

Begin with 6 stitches (bordered by reverse stockinette).
Row 1 and 5: K.
Row 2 and all even rows: P.
Row 3: RC2x2, k2.
Row 7: K2, LC2x2.
Repeat rows 1–8 to continue the pattern.

60 Double Braid with Garter Border

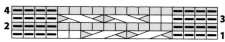

Begin with 18 stitches.
Row 1: P4, (RC2x2) twice, k2, p4.
Row 2 and all even rows: K4, p10, k4.
Row 3: P4, k2, (LC2x2) twice, p4.
Repeat rows 1–4 to continue the pattern.

61 Two over Two Stripes

Begin with a multiple of 6 stitches.
Row 1: P1, (k4, p2) rep across, ending with p1 instead of p2.
Row 2 and all even rows: K1, (p4, k2) rep across, ending with k1 instead of k2.
Row 3: P1, (LC2x2, p2) rep across, ending with p1 instead of p2.
Repeat rows 1–4 to continue the pattern.

62 Offset Stripes

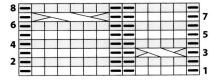

Begin with a multiple of 14 stitches.

Row 1 and 5: P1, (k4, p2, k6, p2) rep across, ending
with p1 instead of p2.

Row 2 and all even rows: K1, (p4, k2, p6, k2) rep across,
ending with k1 instead of k2.

Row 3: P1, (LC2x2, p2, k6, p2) rep across, ending with
p1 instead of p2.

Row 7: P1, (k4, p2, LC3x3, p2) rep across, ending with
p1 instead of p2.

Repeat rows 1–8 to continue the pattern.

63 Large and Small Stripes

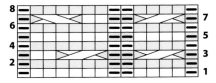

Begin with a multiple of 14 stitches.

Row 1 and 5: P1, (k4, p2, k6, p2) rep across, ending
with p1 instead of p2.

Row 2 and all even rows: K1, (p6, k2, p4, k2) rep across,
ending with k1 instead of k2.

Row 3: P1, (RC2x2, p2, RC2x2, k2, p2) rep across,
ending with p1 instead of p2.

Row 7: P1, (RC2x2, p2, k2, LC2x2, p2) rep across,
ending with p1 instead of p2.

Repeat rows 1–8 to continue the pattern.

64 Cables and Ribs

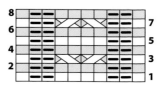

Begin with a multiple of 10 stitches.

Row 1 and 5: K1, (p2, k4, p2, k2) rep across, ending
    with k1 instead of k2.

Row 2 and all even rows: P1, (k2, p4, k2, p2) rep across,
    ending with p1 instead of p2.

Row 3 and 7: K1, (p2, RC1x1, LC1x1, p2, k2) rep across,
    ending with k1 instead of k2.

Repeat rows 1–8 to continue the pattern.

65 All Over Keyholes

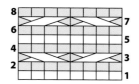

Begin with a multiple of 8 stitches.

Row 1 and 5: K.

Row 2 and all even rows: P.

Row 3: (RC2x2, LC2x2) rep across.

Row 7: (LC2x2, RC2x2) rep across.

Repeat rows 1–8 to continue the pattern.

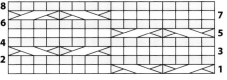

66 Offset Keyholes

Begin with a multiple of 16 stitches.
Row 1: (RC2x2, LC2x2, K8) rep across.
Row 2 and all even rows: P.
Row 3: (K8, RC2x2, LC2x2) rep across.
Row 5: (LC2x2, RC2x2, K8) rep across.
Row 7: (K8, LC2x2, RC2x2) rep across.
Repeat rows 1–8 to continue the pattern.

67 Cable Waves

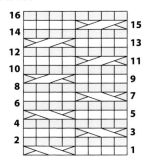

Begin with a multiple of 8 stitches.
Row 1 and 5: (K4, LC2x2) rep across.
Row 2 and all even rows: P.
Row 3 and 7: (LC2x2, k4) rep across.
Row 9 and 13: (K4, RC2x2) rep across.
Row 11 and 15: (RC2x2, k4) rep across.
Repeat rows 1–15 to continue the pattern.

68 All Over Braid

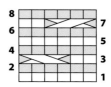

Begin with a multiple of 6 stitches.
Row 1 and 5: K.
Row 2 and all even rows: P
Row 3: (K2, LC2x2) rep across.
Row 7: (RC2x2, k2) rep across.
Repeat rows 1–8 to continue the pattern.

69 Garter Ridge Twist

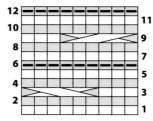

Begin with a multiple of 9 stitches.
Row 1, 5, 6, 7, 11 and 12: K.
Row 2, 4, 8 and 10: P
Row 3: (K3, LC3x3) rep across.
Row 7: (RC3x3, k3) rep across.
Repeat rows 1–8 to continue the pattern.

70 Bobbles and Cables

Begin with 19 stitches.

Row 1 and 17: P4, k4, p1, k1, p1, k4, p4.
Row 2 and 16: K4, p4, k1, p1, k1, p4, k4.
Row 3: P4, RC2xp2, p1, k1, p1, LCp2x2, p4.
Row 4 and 14: K4, p2, k3, p1, k3, p2, k4.
Row 5: P2, RC2xp2, p2, k1, MB, k1, p2, LCp2x2, p2.
Row 6 and 12: K2, p2, k3, p5, k3, p2, k2.
Row 7: RC2x2, p2, k2, MB, k1, MB, k2, p2, LC2x2.
Row 8 and 10: P4, k2, p7, k2, p4.
Row 9: K4, p2, (k1, MB) rep three times, k1, p2, k4.
Row 11: LC2xp2, p2, k2, MB, k1, MB, k2, p2, RC2xp2.
Row 13: P2, LC2xp2, p2, k1, MB, k1, p2, RC2xp2, p2.
Row 15: P4, LC2x2, p1, k1, p1, RC2x2, p4.
Repeat rows 1–16 to continue the pattern.

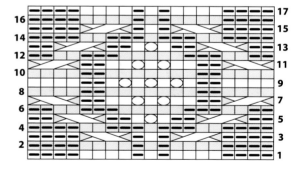

71 Twist within a Cable

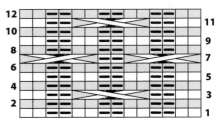

Begin with 14 stitches (bordered by reverse stockinette).

Row 1, 5, and 9: (K2, p2) rep to last two sts, k2.

Row 2 and all even rows: (P2, k2) rep to last two sts,
p2.

Row 3 and 11: K2, p2, LC2x4, p2, k2.

Row 7: RC2x4, p2, RC2x4.

Repeat rows 1–12 to continue the pattern.

72 Back and Forth

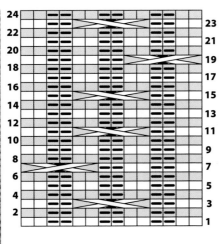

Begin with a multiple of 14
stitches.

Row 1, 5, 9, 13, 17 and 21:
(K2, p2) rep to last two sts, k2.

Row 2 and all even rows: (P2, k2)
rep to last two sts, p2.

Row 3, 11, 15 and 23: K2, p2,
LC2x4/k2xp2, p2, k2.

Row 7: (K2, p2) twice,
RC2x4/p2k2.

Row 19: RC2x4/p2k2), (p2, k2)
twice.

Repeat rows 1–24 to continue
the pattern.

73 Scalloped Border

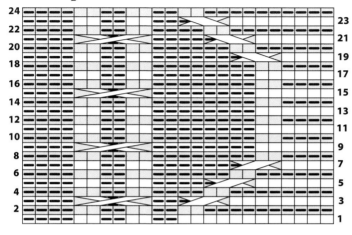

Begin with a multiple of 24 stitches.

Row 1: K12, (p2, k2) twice, p4.

Row 2 and 24: K4, (p2, k2) twice, p2, k10.

Row 3: K8, RC2xp2, p2, RC2x4/p2k2, p4.

Row 4 and 22: K4, p2, k2, p2, k4, p2, k8.

Row 5: K6, RC2xp2, p4, k2, p2, k2, p4.

Row 6 and 20: K4, p2, k2, p2, k6, p2, k6.

Row 7: K4, RC2xp2, p6, k2, p2, k2, p4.

Row 8, 10, 12, 14, 16, 18: K4, p2, k2, p2, k8, p2, k4.

Row 9 and 15: K6, p8, RC2x4/p2k2, p4.

Row 19: K4, LCp2x2, p6, k2, p2, k2, p4.

Row 21: K6, LCp2x2, p4, RC2x4/p2k2, p4.

Row 5: K8, LCp2x2, p2, k2, p2, k2, p4.

Repeat rows 1–24 to continue the pattern.

Embroidery
74 Swiss Darning/Duplicate Stitch

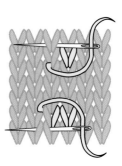

75 Elongated Swiss Darning

76 Straight Stitch

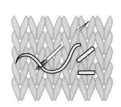

77 Satin Stitch

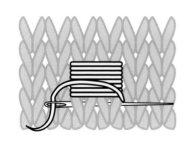

78 Back Stitch

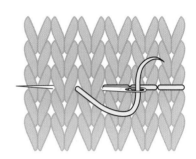

79 Stem Stitch

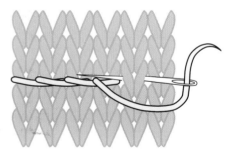

80 Buttonhole Stitch

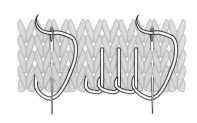

81 Open Cretan

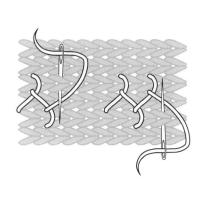

82 Feather Stitch

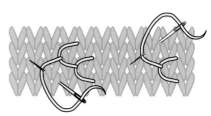

83 Lazy Daisy Stitch

84 Chain Stitch

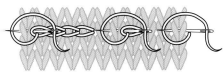

85 French Knot

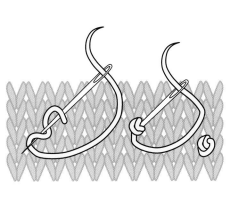

Smocking

The following embroidery patterns are all shown worked in one, two or three rows across a section of knitting. These can be done to gather a section of knitting, or they can be worked all over the knitting, creating a textured surface. To make a swatch for patterns 86 through 99, cast on a multiple of 4 stitches, plus 1, then knit about 30 rows in stockinette stitch. Pre-gather the knitting and review the how-to for smocking in the Basics section, pages 64–72.

86 Stem Stitch

 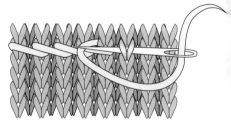

87 Cable Stitch

 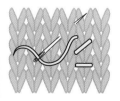 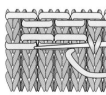

88 Double Cable

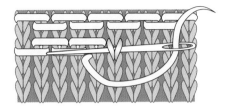 

89 Wave

90 Trellis

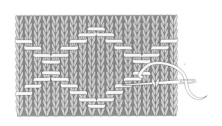 

91 Double Feather

92 Van Dyke

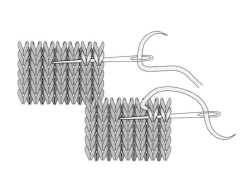

Diamond Smocking

For patterns 93 through 98, knit the pattern indicated. Pre-gather the knitting if instructed. Then, following the numbering on the chart, begin with the embroidery yarn coming out on the left of number 1, embroider the knitting with the steps below, inserting the needle behind every stitch from right to left.

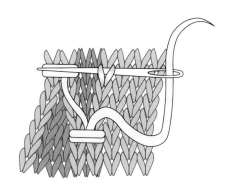

1. Pass behind 2 and 1.
2. Pass behind 2.
3. Pass behind 3.
4. Pass behind 4 and 3.
5. Pass behind 4.
6. Pass behind 5.
Stitch number 5 becomes stitch number 1. Repeat step 1 through 6 across the rows of knitting.

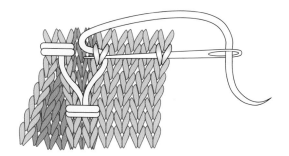

93 Diamond

Begin with a multiple of 4 stitches, plus 1.
Row 1: K.
Row 2: P.
Repeat row 1 and 2 a multiple of 10 times.
Pre-gather every fourth column of knitting.

94 Diamond on Seed Stitch

Begin with a multiple of 4 stitches, plus 1
Row 1: (P1, k1) rep to last st, p1.
Rep row 1 a multiple of 6 times.
Pre-gather every fourth column of knitting.

95 Diamond on Ribbing

Begin with a multiple of 3 stitches, plus 1
Row 1: (K1, p2) rep to last st, k1.
Row 2: (P1, k2) rep to last st, p1.
Repeat row 1 and 2 a multiple of 3 times.
No need to pre-gather.

96 Diamond on Dotted Rib

Begin with a multiple of 4 stitches, plus 1.
Row 1: (K1, p3) rep to last st, k1.
Row 2: K.
Repeat row 1 and 2 a multiple of 6 times.
No need to pre-gather.

97 Diamond on Cables

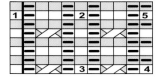

Begin with a multiple of 5 stitches, plus 1
Row 1: (K1, p1, RC1x1, p1) rep to last st, k1.
Row 2 and 4: (P1, k1, p2, k1) rep to last st, p1.
Row 3: (K1, p1, k2, p1) rep to last st, k1.
Repeat row 1 - 4 a multiple of 6 times.
No need to pre-gather.

98 Diamond on Lace

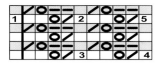

Begin with a multiple of 5 stitches plus 1
Row 1: K1, (k2tog, yo, k3) rep across.
Row 2: P1, (k2tog, yo, k2, p1) rep across.
Repeat row 1 and 2 a multiple of 3 times.
No need to pre-gather.

Dimensional
99 Dropped Stitch

Begin with a multiple of 2 stitches plus 1.
Row 1 and 2: K.
Row 3: K1, (yo, k1) rep across.
Row 4: K1, (drp 1, k1) rep across.
Repeat rows 1–4 to continue the pattern.

100 Diamond Dropped Stitch

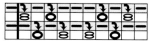

Begin with a multiple of 10 stitches plus 1.
Row 1: K2, (yo, (k1, yo, yo) twice, k1, yo, k3) rep across,
ending with k2 instead of k3.
Row 2: K2, (drp 1, k1, (drp 2, k1) twice, drp 1, k3) rep
across, ending with k2 instead of k3.
Row 3: K1, (yo, yo, k1, yo, k3, yo, k1, yo, yo, k2) rep
across, ending with k1 instead of k2.
Row 4: K1, (drp 2, k1, drp 1, k3, drp 1, k1, drp 2, k2) rep
across, ending with k1 instead of k2.
Repeat rows 1–4 to continue the pattern.

101 Undulating Drop Stitch Stripes

Multiple of 8 stitches plus 1

Row 1: K2, (yo, (k1, yo, yo) rep 4 times, k1, yo, k3) rep across, ending with k2 instead of k3.

Row 2: K2, (drp 1, k1, (drp 2, k1) rep 4 times, drp 1, k3) rep across, ending with k2 instead of k3.

Row 3 and 4: K.

Row 5: K1, (yo, yo, k1, yo, k5, yo, k1, yo, yo, k1) rep across.

Row 6: K1, (drp 2, k1, drp 1, k5, drp 1, k1, drp 2, k1) rep across.

Row 7, 9, 11 and 12: K.

Row 8 and 10: P.

Repeat rows 1–12 to continue the pattern.

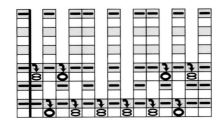

102 Bobble Edging

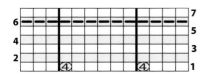

Begin with a multiple of 6 stitches plus 7.

Row 1: K3, ((k1, p1, k1, p1) into next st, making 4 sts
from one. Working only in the 4 new sts, turn, p
across 4 sts, turn, k across 4 sts, turn, p across 4 sts,
turn, k4tog. K5) rep across, ending with k3 instead
of k5.

Row 2–5: Work in St st.

Row 6 and 7: K.

BO in k st.

103 Bobble Stripes

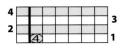

Begin with a multiple of 6 stitches plus 1.

MB (Make Bobble): (K1, p1, k1, p1) into next st, making 4 sts from one. Working only in the 4 new sts, turn, p across 4 sts, turn, k across 4 sts, turn, p across 4 sts, turn, k4tog.

Row 1: K5, (MB, k6) rep across, ending with k1, instead of k6.

Row 2 and all even rows: P.

Row 3: K.

Repeat rows 1–4 to continue the pattern.

104 All Over Bobbles

Begin with a multiple of 5 stitches, plus 2.

MB (Make Bobble): K into the front and back of the next st twice, making 4 sts from one. Working only in the 4 new sts, turn, p across 4 sts, turn k across 4 sts, pass 3 sts over first st on right needle.

Row 1: K2, (MB, k5) rep across, ending with k2 instead of k5.

Row 2 and all even rows: P.

Row 3: K.

Row 5: K5, (MB, k5) rep across.

Repeat rows 1–6 to continue the pattern.

105 Bobble Clusters

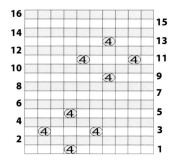

Begin with a multiple of 10 stitches.

MB (Make Bobble): (K1, p1, k1, p1) into next st, making 4 sts from one. Working only in the 4 new sts, turn, p across 4 sts, turn, k across 4 sts, turn, p across 4 sts, turn, k4tog.

Row 1 and 5: K6, (MB, k9) rep across, ending with k3, instead of k9.

Row 2 and all even rows: P.

Row 3: K4, (MB, k3, MB, k5) rep across, ending with k1 instead of k5.

Row 7 and 15: K.

Row 9 and 13: K3, (MB, k9) rep across, ending with k6, instead of k9.

Row 11: K1, (MB, k3, MB, k5) rep across, ending with k4, instead of k5.

Repeat rows 1–12 to continue the pattern.

106 ZigZag and Bobbles

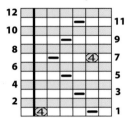

Begin with a multiple of 6 stitches plus 1.

MB (Make Bobble): (K1, p1, k1, p1) into next st, making 4 sts from one. Working only in the 4 new sts, turn, p across 4 sts, turn, k across 4 sts, turn, p across 4 sts, turn, k4tog.

Row 1: (K1, p1, k3, MB) rep to last st, k1.

Row 2 and all even rows: P.

Row 3 and 11: K2, (p1, k5) rep across, ending with k4 instead of k5.

Row 5 and 9, K3, (p1, k5) rep across, ending with k3 instead of k5.

Row 7: K1, (MB, k2, p1, k2) rep across.

Repeat rows 1–10 to continue the pattern.

107 Eyelet Vine and Bobbles

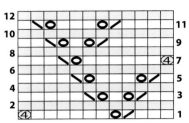

Begin with a multiple of 12 stitches.

MB (Make Bobble): (K1, p1, k1, p1) into next st,
making 4 sts from one. Working only in the 4 new
sts, turn, p across 4 sts, turn, k across 4 sts, turn, p
across 4 sts, turn, k4tog.

Row 1: (K3, k2tog, yo, k6, MB) rep across.

Row 2 and all even rows: P.

Row 3: K2, (k2tog, yo, k1, yo, SKP, k7) rep across,
ending with k5 instead of k7.

Row 5: K1, (k2tog, yo, k3, yo, SKP, k5) rep across,
ending with k4 instead of k5.

Row 7: (MB, k6, yo, SKP, k3) rep across.

Row 9: K5, (k2tog, yo, k1, yo, SKP, k7) rep across,
ending with k2, instead of k7.

Row 11: K4, (k2tog, yo, k3, yo, SKP, k5) rep across,
ending with k1 instead of k5.

Repeat rows 1–12 to continue the pattern.

108 Bobble on Sprigs

Begin with a multiple of 19 stitches.

MB (Make Bobble): (K1, p1, k1, p1) into next st, making 4 sts from one. Working only in the 4 new sts, turn, p across 4 sts, turn, k across 4 sts, turn, p across 4 sts, turn, k4tog.

Row 1: K1, (k2tog, k4, yo, (k1, p1) twice, k1, yo, k4, SKP, k2) rep across, ending with k1, instead of k2.

Row 2 and all even rows: P.

Row 3: K1, (k2tog, k3, yo, k1, MB, p1, k1, p1, MB, k1, yo, k3, SKP, k2) rep across, ending with k1, instead of k2.

Row 5: K1, (k2tog, k2, yo, k1, MB, (k1, p1) twice, k1, MB, k1, yo, k2, SKP, k2) rep across, ending with k1, instead of k2.

Row 7: K1, (k2tog, k1, yo, k1, MB, k2, p1, k1, p1, k2, MB, k1, yo, k1, SKP, k2) rep across, ending with k1, instead of k2.

Row 9: K1, (k2tog, yo, k1, MB, k3 p1, k1, p1, k3, MB, k1, yo, SKP, k2) rep across, ending with k1, instead of k2.

Row 11: K2, (MB, k5, p1, k1, p1, k5, MB, k4) rep across, ending with k2, instead of k2.

Repeat rows 1–12 to continue the pattern.

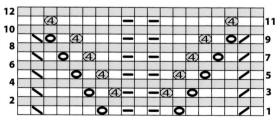

109 Bobble Wave

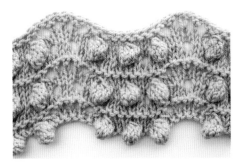

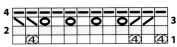

Begin with a multiple of 12 stitches.

MB (Make Bobble): (K1, p1, k1, p1) into next st, making 4 sts from one. Working only in the 4 new sts, turn, p across 4 sts, turn, k across 4 sts, turn, p across 4 sts, turn, k4tog.

Row 1: (MB, k1, MB, k7, MB, k1) rep across.

Row 2: P.

Row 3: (K1, (K2tog) twice, (yo, k1) rep 3 times, yo, (SKP) twice) rep across.

Row 4: K.

Repeat rows 1–4 to continue the pattern.

110 Ruffle

Begin with any number of stitches, increasing to twice as many.

Row 1: K.

Row 2: P.

Row 3: M1 in ea st.

Row 4: P.

Row 5–8: K.

BO.

111 Shallow Ruffle

Begin with a multiple of 2 stitches, increasing to multiple of 3.

Row 1: K.

Row 2: P.

Row 3: (K1, M1) rep across.

Row 4: P.

Row 5–8: K.

BO.

112 Full Lacy Ruffle

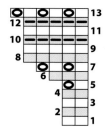

Begin with a multiple of 2 stitches, increasing to multiple of 6.

Row 1, 3, and 9 through 12: K.

Row 2, 4, 6 and 8: P.

Row 5, 7 and 13: (K1, yo) rep across.

BO.

113 Open Lace Ruffle

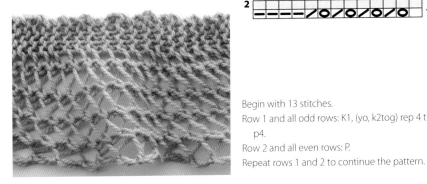

Begin with 13 stitches.
Row 1 and all odd rows: K1, (yo, k2tog) rep 4 times, p4.
Row 2 and all even rows: P.
Repeat rows 1 and 2 to continue the pattern.

114 Pointed Lace Ruffle

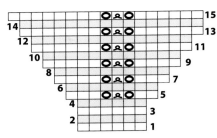

Begin with a multiple of 6 stitches.
Row 1 and 3: K.
Row 2 and all even rows: P.
Row 5: K2, (yo, k1 tbl, yo, k5) rep across, ending with k3 instead of k5.
Row 7: K3, (yo, k1 tbl, yo, k7) rep across, ending with k4 instead of k7.
Row 9: K4, (yo, k1 tbl, yo, k9) rep across, ending with k5 instead of k9.
Row 11: K5, (yo, k1 tbl, yo, k11) rep across, ending with k6 instead of k11.

Row 13: K6, (yo, k1 tbl, yo, k13) rep across, ending with k7 instead of k13.
Row 15: K7, (yo, k1 tbl, yo, k15) rep across, ending with k8 instead of k15.
Repeat rows 1–16 to continue the pattern.

115 Crochet Edged Ruffle

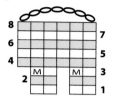

Begin with a multiple of 4 stitches, increasing to a
   multiple of 6.

Row 1: K.

Row 2, 4, 6, and 8: P.

Row 3: (K1, M1) rep across.

Row 5 and 7: K.

Repeat rows 1–8 to continue pattern.

To BO, using a crochet hook, *pick up the next 6 sts,
   yo, pull through all sts, ch 8, rep from * across row

116 Double Gathered Ruffle

Any number of stitches.

Row 1–2: K.

Row 3: Working in stockinette st, M 1
   in ea st–twice the number of sts.

Row 4: P.

Row –5–8: Wk in St st.

Row 9: (K2tog) rep across.

Row 10: K.

Rows 11–18 Repeat rows 1–8.

Row 19: K.

BO.

117 Eyelet and Ribbon

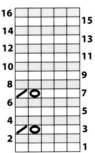

Begin with a multiple of 5 stitches.

Row 1, 5, 9, 11, 13, and 15: K.

Row 2 and all even rows: P.

Row 3 and 7: (K3, yo, k2tog) rep across.

BO, thread ribbon through eyelet holes and gather to
    desired size.

118 Simple Leaf

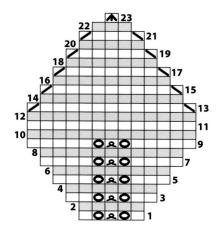

CO 3 sts and work I-cord for 12 rows or desired length for leaf stem.

Make leaf as foll:

Row 1: K1, yo, k1ib, yo, k1.

Row 2 and all even rows: P.

Row 3: K2, yo, k1ib, yo, k2.

Row 5: K3, yo, k1ib, yo, k3.

Row 7: K4, yo, k1ib, yo, k4.

Row 9: K5, yo, k1ib, yo, k5.

Row 11: K.

Row 13 through row 21: SKP, k to last 2 sts, k2tog.

Row 23: K3tog.

119 Three Point Leaf

CO 3 sts and work I-cord for 12 rows or desired length for leaf stem.

Make leaf as foll:

Row 1: K1, yo, k1ib, yo, k1.

Row 2 and all even rows: P.

Row 3: K2, yo, k1ib, yo, k2.

Row 5: K3, yo, k1ib, yo, k3.

Row 7: K4, yo, k1ib, yo, k4.

Row 9: K5, yo, k1ib, yo, k5.

Row 11: K6, yo, k1ib, yo, k6.

Row 13: K7, yo, k1ib, yo, k7.

Row 15: K8, yo, k1ib, yo, k8.

Row 16: BO 5 sts at beg of row, p rem sts, leaving 14 sts remaining.

Row 17: BO 5 sts at beg of row, k1, psso, k to last two sts, k2tog, leaving 9 sts remaining.

Row 19 through row 21: SKP, k to last 2 sts, k2tog.

Row 23: K3tog.

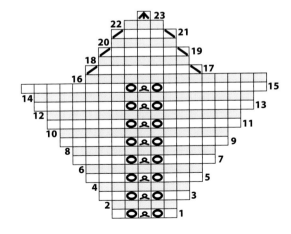

120 Four-Stitch I-Cord

Begin with a multiple of 4 stitches on two dpn.
Row 1: K, do not turn.
Row 2 and all rows: With the right side still facing,
    slide the knitting to the right end of the needle,
    bring the working yarn around the back of the
    knitting and k across the row, do not turn.

To BO, cut the yarn to 6" and pass
    through all 4 sts.

121 I-Cord Dots

Begin with 4 stitches on two dpn.
Row 1: K2, p1, k1, do not turn.
Row 2 and all rows: With the right side still facing,
    slide the knitting to the right end of the needle,
    bring the working yarn around the back of the
    knitting, k2, p1, k1, do not turn

To BO, cut the yarn to 6" and pass
    through all 4 sts.

121 I-Cord Purl

Begin with a multiple of 4 stitches on two dpn.
Row 1: P, do not turn.
Row 2 and all rows: With the right side still facing,
    slide the knitting to the right end of the needle,
    bring the working yarn around the back of the
    knitting and p across the row, do not turn.

To BO, cut the yarn to 6" and pass
    through all 4 sts.

123 I-Cord Bobble

Begin with a multiple of 4 stitches on two dpn.

Row 1: K2, MB, k1, do not turn.

Row 2 and 3: With the right side still facing, slide the knitting to the right end of the needle, bring the working yarn around the back of the knitting, k across the row, do not turn.

Row 4: With the right side still facing, slide the knitting to the right end of the needle, bring the working yarn around the back of the knitting, k2, MB, k1, do not turn.

Rep row 2, 3 and 4.

To BO, cut the yarn to 6" and pass through all 4 sts.

124 I-Cord Beads

Pre-string any number of beads onto the yarn.

Begin with a multiple of 4 stitches on two dpn.

Row 1: K1, p1, B1, p1, k1, do not turn.

Row 2 and 3: With the right side still facing, slide the knitting to the right end of the needle, bring the working yarn around the back of the knitting, k across the row, do not turn.

Row 4: With the right side still facing, slide the knitting to the right end of the needle, bring the working yarn around the back of the knitting, k1, p1, B1, p1, k1, do not turn.

Rep row 2, 3 and 4.

To BO, cut the yarn to 6" and pass through all 4 sts.

Eyelets
125 Eyelet Dots

Begin with a multiple of 4 stitches, plus 1.
Row 1: (K2tog, yo, k2) rep to last st, k1.
Row 2 and all even rows: P.
Row 3: K.
Row 5: (K2, k2tog, yo) rep to last st, k1.
Repeat rows 1–6 to continue the pattern.

126 Threes

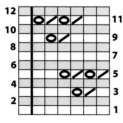

Begin with a multiple of 6 stitches, plus 1.
Row 1: K.
Row 2 and all even rows: P.
Row 3: K1, (k2tog, yo, k4) rep across.
Row 5: ((K2tog, yo) twice, k2) rep across.
Row 7: K.
Row 9: K3, (k2tog, yo, k4) rep across, ending with k2 instead of k4.
Row 11: K2, ((k2tog, yo) twice, k2) rep across, ending with k1 instead of k3.
Repeat rows 1–12 to continue the pattern.

127 Eyelet Rows

Begin with a multiple of 4 stitches, plus 1.
Row 1: (K2tog, yo, k2) rep to last st, k1.
Row 2, 4 and 8: P.
Row 3: (K2, k2tog, yo) rep to last st, k1.
Row 5, 6 and 7: K.
Repeat rows 1–8 to continue the pattern.

128 Eyelet Clusters

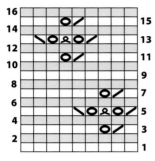

Begin with a multiple of 6 stitches, plus 3.

Row 1: K.

Row 2 and all even rows: P.

Row 3: K1, (k2tog, yo, k4) rep to last 3 sts, k2.

Row 5: (K2tog, yo, kib, yo, SKP, k1) rep to last 3 sts, k3.

Row 7: K1, (k2tog, yo, k4) rep to last 3 sts, k2.

Row 9: K.

Row 11: K4, (k2tog, yo, k4) rep across, except on the last rep, end with k3 instead of k4.

Row 13: K3, (K2tog, yo, kib, yo, SKP, k1), rep across.

Row 15: K4, (k2tog, yo, k4) rep across, except on the last rep, end with k3 instead of k4.

Repeat rows 1–16 to continue the pattern.

129 Eyelet Checkerboard

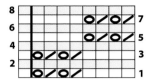

Begin with a multiple of 8 stitches, plus 1.
Row 1 and 3: (K4, (k2tog, yo) twice) rep across.
Row 2 and all even rows: P.
Row 5 and 7: ((Ktog, yo) twice, k4) rep across.
Repeat rows 1–8 to continue the pattern.

130 Eyelet Fans

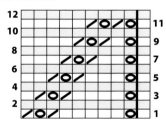

Begin with a multiple of 9 stitches, plus 1
Row 1: K1, (yo, k5, k2tog, yo, k2tog) rep across.
Row 2 and all even rows: P.
Row 3: K1, (yo, k4, k2tog, yo, k2tog, k1) rep across.
Row 5: K1, (yo, k3, k2tog, yo, k2tog, k2) rep across.
Row 7: K1, (yo, k2, k2tog, yo, k2tog, k3) rep across.
Row 9: K1, (yo, k1, k2tog, yo, k2tog, k4) rep across.
Row 11: K1, ((yo, k2tog) twice, k5) rep across.
Repeat rows 1–12 to continue the pattern.

131 Eyelet Branches

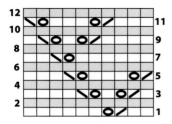

Begin with a multiple of 10 stitches.

Row 1: K2, (k2tog, yo, k8) rep across, ending with k6 instead of k8.

Row 2 and all even rows: P.

Row 3: K1, (k2tog, yo, k1, yo, SKP, k5) rep across, ending with k4 instead of k5.

Row 5: (K2tog, yo, k3, yo, SKP, k3) rep across.

Row 7: K6, (yo, SKP, k8) rep across, ending with k2 instead of k8.

Row 9: K4, (k2tog, yo, k1, yo, SKP, k5) rep across, ending with k1 instead of k5.

Row 11: (K3, k2tog, yo, k3, yo, SKP) rep across.

Repeat rows 1–12 to continue the pattern.

132 Eyelet Stripes

Begin with a multiple of 10 stitches.

Row 1: K1 (yo, k2, SKP, k2tog, k2, yo, k2) rep across, ending with k1 instead of k2.

Row 2 and all even rows: P.

Repeat rows 1 and 2 to continue the pattern.

133 Eyelet Sway

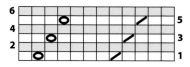

Begin with a multiple of 12 stitches.

Row 1: K4, (k2tog, k5, yo, k5) rep across, ending with k1, instead of k5.

Row 2 and all even rows: P.

Row 3: K3, (k2tog, k5, yo, k5) rep across, ending with k2 instead of k5.

Row 5: K2, (k2tog, k5, yo, k5) rep across, ending with k3 instead of k5.

Repeat rows 1–6 to continue the pattern.

134 Eyelet Wheat Stalks

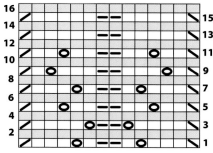

Begin with a multiple of 14 stitches.

Row 1 and 7: (SKP, k3, yo, k1, p2, k1, yo, k3, k2tog) rep across.

Row 2 and all even rows: P.

Row 3: (SKP, k4, yo, p2, yo, k4, k2tog) rep across.

Row 5 and 11: (SKP, k2, yo, k2, p2, k2, yo, k2, k2tog) rep across..

Row 9: (SKP, k1, yo, k3, p2, k3, yo, k1, k2tog) rep across.

Row 13 and 15: (SKP, k5, p2, k5, k2tog) rep across.

Repeat rows 1–16 to continue the pattern.

135 Eyelet Mini Wave

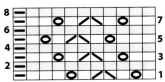

Begin with a multiple of 11 stitches
Row 1: (K1, yo, k1, SKP, k2tog, k1, yo, k3, p1) rep across.
Row 2 and all even rows: P.
Row 3 and 7: (K2, yo, k1, SKP, k2tog, k1, yo, k2, p1) rep
    across.
Row 5: (K3, yo, k1, SKP, k2tog, k1, yo, k1, p1) rep across.
Repeat rows 1–8 to continue the pattern.

136 Eyelet Fountains

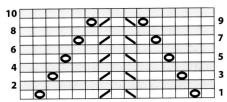

Worked from the top down, multiple of 15 stitches.
Row 1: K1, (yo, k4, SKP, k1, k2tog, k4, yo, k2) rep across, ending with k1 instead of k2.
Row 2 and all even rows: P.
Row 3: K2, (yo, k3, SKP, k1, k2tog, k3, yo, k4) rep across, ending with k2 instead of k4.
Row 5: K3, (yo, k2, SKP, k1, k2tog, k2, yo, k6) rep across, ending with k3 instead of k6.
Row 7: K4, (yo, k1, SKP, k1, k2tog, k1, yo, k8) rep across, ending with k4 instead of k8.
Row 9: K5, (yo, SKP, k1, k2tog, yo, k10) rep across, ending with k5 instead of k10.
Repeat rows 1–10 to continue the pattern.

137 Eyelet Palm

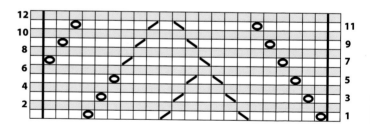

Begin with a multiple of 22 stitches, plus 2.

Row 1: K1, (yo, k5, SKP, k5, k2tog, k5, yo, k3) rep to last st, k1.

Row 2 and all even rows: P.

Row 3: K2, (yo, k5, SKP, k3, k2tog, k5, yo, k5) rep across.

Row 5: K3, (yo, k5, SKP, k1, k2tog, k5, yo, k7) rep across, ending with k6 instead of k7.

Row 7: K4, (yo, k5, SKP, k5, k2tog, k5, yo, k3) rep across, ending with k1 instead of k3.

Row 9: K5, (yo, k5, SKP, k3, k2tog, k5, yo, k5) rep across, ending with k2 instead of k5.

Row 11: K6, (yo, k5, SKP, k1, k2tog, k5, yo, k7) rep across, ending with k3, instead of k7.

Repeat rows 1–12 to continue the pattern.

138 ZigZag Garter Border

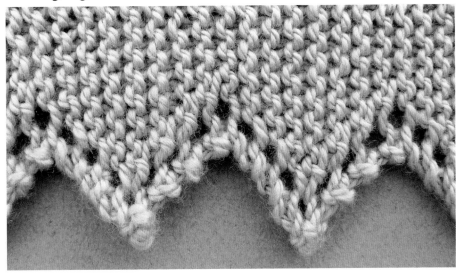

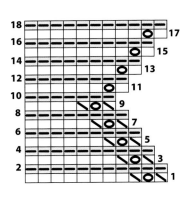

Begin with a multiple of 11 stitches.
Row 1: SKP, yo, SKP, k8.
Row 2 and all even rows: K.
Row 3: SKP, yo, SKP, k7.
Row 5: SKP, yo, SKP, k6.
Row 7: SKP, yo, SKP, k5.
Row 9: SKP, yo, SKP, k4.
Row 11: K1, yo, k6.
Row 13: K1, yo, k7
Row 15: K1, yo, k8
Row 17: K1, yo, k9.
Rep rows 1–18 to continue the pattern.

139 Eyelet Triangle Edge

Begin with a multiple of 12 stitches, plus 1.

Row 1: K.

Row 2 and all even rows: P.

Row 3: (K2tog, yo) rep to last st, k1.

Row 5: K3, ((k2tog, yo) three times, k6) rep across, ending with k4 instead of k6.

Row 7: K4, ((k2tog, yo) twice, k8) rep across, ending with k5, instead of k8.

Row 9: K5, (k2tog, yo, k10) rep across, ending with k6 instead of k10.

Row 11 and 13: K.

BO.

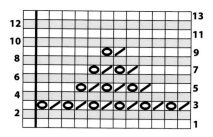

140 Eyelet Posy Border

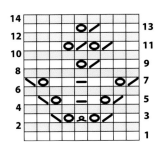

Begin with a multiple of 9 stitches.

Row 1 and 14: K.

Row 2 and all even rows through row 12: P.

Row 3: K2, k2tog, yo, kib, yo, SKP, k2.

Row 5: K1, k2tog, yo, k1, p1, k1, yo, SKP, k1.

Row 7: K2tog, yo, k2, p1, k2, yo, SKP.

Row 9 and 13: K3, k2tog, yo, k4.

Row 11: K2, (k2tog, yo) twice, k3.

Row 13: K3, k2tog, yo, k4

Row 15: P.

BO.

141 Leaf Border

Begin with a multiple of 14 stitches, plus 1.

Row 1: (K4, k2tog, yo, k4, yo, SKP, k2tog, yo) rep to
last st, k1.

Row 2 and all even rows: P.

Row 3: (K3, k2tog, yo, k1, yo, SKP, k2, yo, SKP, k2tog,
yo) rep to last st, k1.

Row 5: (K2, k2tog, yo, k3, yo, SKP, yo, SKP, k2tog, yo)
rep to last st, k1.

Row 7: (K1, k2tog, yo, k5, (yo, SKP) twice, k2tog, yo)
rep to last st, k1.

Row 9: (K3, yo, k1, k3tog, k1, yo, k2, yo, SKP, k2tog,
yo) rep to last st, k1.

Row 11: (K4, yo, k3tog, yo, k3, yo, SKP, k2tog, yo) rep
to last st, k1.

Row 13, 14 and 15: K.

BO.

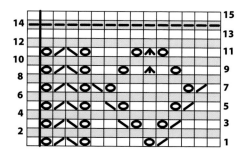

Lace

142 Lace Open Stripes

Begin with a multiple of 4 stitches.
Row 1: (K2tog, yo, k2) rep across.
Rep Row 1 to continue the pattern.

143 Lace Rib

Begin with a multiple of 5 stitches.
Row 1: (K2tog, yo, k3) rep across.
Row 2: (P1, p2tog, yo, p2) rep across.
Repeat rows 1 and 2 to continue the pattern.

144 Lace Dots

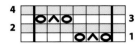

Begin with a multiple of 6 stitches, plus 2.

Row 1: K1, (yo, k3tog, yo, k3) rep to the last 7 sts, yo, k3tog, yo, k4.

Row 2 and all even rows: P.

Row 3: K4, (yo, k3tog, yo, k3) rep to the last 4 sts, yo, k3tog, yo, k1.

Repeat rows 1–4 to continue the pattern.

145 Lace Swaying

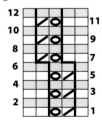

Begin with a multiple of 2 stitches,
    plus 3.

Row 1, 3 and 5: K1, (k2tog, yo) rep to last 2 sts, k2.

Row 2 and all even rows: P.

Row 7, 9 and 11: K2, (yo, k2tog) rep to last st, k1.

Repeat rows 1–12 to continue the pattern.

146 Lace ZigZag

Begin with a multiple of 5 stitches.
Row 1: K2, (yo, SKP, k3) rep across,
   ending with k1 instead of k3.
Row 2 and all even rows: P.
Row 3: (K3, yo, SKP) rep across.
Row 5: K1, (k2tog, yo, k3) rep across, ending with k2
   instead of k3.
Row 7 (K2tog, yo, k3) rep across.
Repeat rows 1–8 to continue the pattern.

147 Lace Wave Stripe

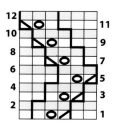

Begin with a multiple of 3 stitches, plus 3.
Row 1: K2, (k2tog, yo, k1) rep to the last st, k1.
Row 2 and all even rows: P.
Row 3: K1, (k2tog, yo, k1) rep to the last 2 sts, k2.
Row 5: (K2tog, yo, k1) rep to the last 3 sts, k3.
Row 7: K1, (k1, yo, SKP) rep to the last 2 sts, k2.
Row 9: K2, (k1, yo, SKP) rep to the last st, k1.
Row 11: K3, (k1, yo, SKP) rep across.
Repeat rows 1–12 to continue the pattern.

148 Lace Offset Triangle

Begin with a multiple of 9 stitches, plus 1.

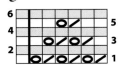

Row 1: (K3, (k2tog, yo) three times) rep to last st, k1.

Row 2 and all even rows: P.

Row 3: K4, ((k2tog, yo) twice, k5) rep across, ending with k2 instead of k5

Row 5: K5, (k2tog, yo, k7) rep across, ending with k3 instead of k7.

Row 7: ((K2tog, yo) three times, k3) rep across, ending with k4 instead of k3.

Row 9: K1, ((k2tog, yo) twice, k5) rep across.

Row 11: K2, (k2tog, yo, k7) rep across, ending with k6 instead of k7.

Repeat rows 1–12 to continue the pattern.

149 Lace Triangle

Begin with a multiple of 6 stitches, plus 1.

Row 1: (K2tog, yo) rep to last st, k1.

Row 2 and all even rows: P.

Row 3: K1, ((k2tog, yo) twice, k2) rep across.

Row 5: K2, (k2tog, yo, k4) rep across, ending with k3 instead of k4.

Repeat rows 1–6 to continue the pattern.

150 Lace Rope

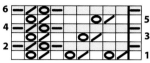

Begin with a multiple of 9 stitches, plus 1
Row 1: K1, (k2tog, yo, k1) rep across.
Row 2 and all even rows: K1, (k2tog, yo, k1, p5, k1) rep
across.
Row 3: K3, (k2tog, yo, k2, k2tog, yo, k3) rep across,
ending with k1, instead of k3.
Row 5: K2, (k2tog, yo, k3, k2tog, yo, k2) rep across,
ending with k1, instead of k2.
Repeat rows 1–6 to continue the pattern.

151 Lace Undulations

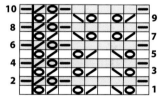

Begin with a multiple of 9 stitches, plus 1
Row 1, 3 and 5: (K1, yo, SKP, k1, k2tog, yo, k1, k2tog,
yo) rep to last st, k1.
Row 2 and all even rows: K1 (k2tog, yo, k1, p5, k1) rep
across.
Row 7 and 9: (K1, k2tog, yo, k1, yo, SKP, k1, k2tog, yo)
rep to last st, k1.
Repeat rows 1–10 to continue the pattern.

152 Lace Delicate Stripes

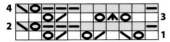

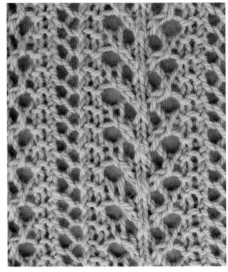

Begin with a multiple of 11 stitches
Row 1: K1, (yo, SKP, k1, k2tog, yo, k1, k2tog, yo, k3) rep
 across, ending with k2, instead of k3.
Row 2 and all even rows: (K2tog, yo, k3, p5, k1).
Row 3: K2, (yo, k3tog, yo, k2, k2tog, yo, k4) rep across,
 ending with k2, instead of k4.
Repeat rows 1–4 to continue the pattern.

153 Large Diamonds

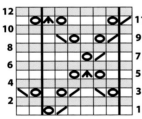

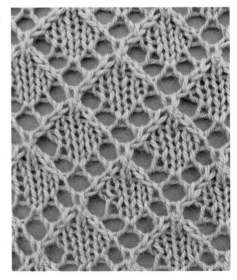

Begin with a multiple of 6 stitches, plus 3.
Row 1: K5, k2tog, yo, (k4, k2tog, yo) rep to last 2 sts, k2.
Row 2 and all even rows: P.
Row 3: K1, (yo, SKP, k1, k2tog, yo, k1) rep to last 2 sts,
 yo, SKP.
Row 5: K2, (yo, k3tog, yo, k3) rep to last st, k1.
Row 7: K2, (k2tog, yo, k4) rep to last st, k1.
Row 9: K1, (k2tog, yo, k1, yo, SKP, k1) rep to last 2 sts, k2.
Row 11: K2tog, yo, (k3, yo, k3tog, yo) rep to last st, k1.
Repeat rows 1–12 to continue the pattern.

154 Lace Small Diamonds

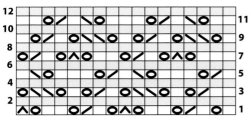

Begin with a multiple of 16 stitches, plus 2.

Row 1: K1, (yo, k1, k2tog, yo, k2, yo, k3tog, yo, k1, k2tog, yo, k2, yo, k3tog) rep to the last st, k1.

Row 2 and all even rows: P.

Row 3: K1, (k1, k2tog, yo, k1, yo, SKP, SKP, yo, k1, k2tog, yo, k1, yo, SKP, SKP, yo) rep to the last st, k1.

Row 5: K1, (k2tog, yo, k3, yo, SKP, k1, k2tog, yo, k3, yo, SKP, k1) rep to the last st, k1.

Row 7: K1, (K2, yo, k3tog, yo, k1, k2tog, yo, k2, yo, k3tog, yo, k1, k2tog, yo) rep to the last st, k1.

Row 9: K1, (yo, SKP, SKP, yo, k1, k2tog, yo, k1, yo, SKP, SKP, yo, k1, k2tog, yo, k1) rep to the last st, k1.

Row 11: K1, (k1, yo, SKP, k1, k2tog, yo, k3, yo, SKP, k1, k2tog, yo, k2) rep to the last st, k1.

Repeat rows 1–12 to continue the pattern.

155 Lace Wave

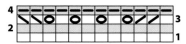

Begin with a multiple of 12 stitches.

Row 1: K.

Row 2: P.

Row 3: (K1, (k2tog) twice, (yo, k1) rep 3 times, yo, (SKP) twice) rep across.

Row 4: K.

Repeat rows 1–4 to continue the pattern.

156 Larkspur

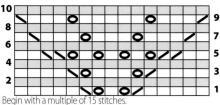

Begin with a multiple of 15 stitches.

Row 1: K5, (k2tog, yo, k1, yo, SKP, k10) rep to the last 10 sts, k2tog, yo, k1, yo, SKP, k5.

Row 2 and all even rows: P.

Row 3: K4, (k2tog, yo, k3, yo, SKP, k8) rep to the last 11 sts, k2tog, yo, k3, yo, SKP, k4.

Row 5: K2, ((K2tog) twice, yo, (k1, yo) rep three times, (SKP) twice, k4) rep to the last 13 sts, (K2tog) twice, yo, (k1, yo) rep three times, (SKP) twice, k2.

Row 7: K1, (k2tog, k3, (yo, k3) twice, SKP, k2) rep to the last 14 sts, k2tog, k3, (yo, k3) twice, SKP, k1.

Row 9: (K2tog, k3, yo, k5, yo, k3, SKP) rep across.

Repeat rows 1–10 to continue the pattern.

157 Lace Leaves

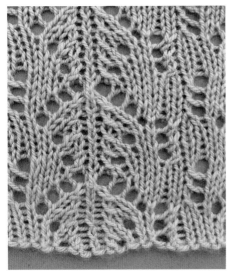

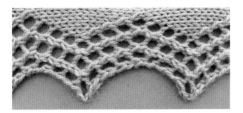

Begin with a multiple of 15 stitches.

CO 45 sts

Row 1: (K2tog, yo, k3, yo, SKP, kib, k2tog, yo, k5) rep across.

Row 2 and all even rows: P.

Row 3: (K2tog, yo, k2, yo, k1, SKP, kib, k2tog, k1, yo, k4) rep across.

Row 5: (K2tog, yo, k1, yo, k2, SKP, kib, k2tog, k1, yo, k3) rep across.

Row 7: (K4, yo, k1, SKP, kip, k2tog, k1, yo, k2, yo, SKP) rep across.

Row 9: (K5, yo, SKP, kip, k2tog, yo, k3, yo, SKP) rep across.

Row 11: (K6, yo, k3tog, yo, k4, yo, SKP) rep across.

Repeat rows 1–12 to continue the pattern.

158 Lace Sawtooth Border

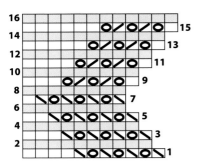

Begin with a multiple of 11 stitches.

Row 1: (SKP, yo) rep 3 times, SKP, k4.

Row 2 and all even rows: P.

Row 3: (SKP, yo) rep 3 times, SKP, k3.

Row 5: (SKP, yo) rep 3 times, SKP, k2.

Row 7: (SKP, yo) rep 3 times, SKP, k1

Row 9: K1, yo, (k2tog, yo) rep twice, k3.

Row 11: K1, yo, (k2tog, yo) rep twice, k4.

Row 13: K1, yo, (k2tog, yo) rep twice, k5.

Row 15: K1, yo, (k2tog, yo) rep twice, k6.

Rep rows 1–16 to continue the pattern.

159 Lace Garter Sawtooth Border

Begin with a multiple of 11 stitches.
Row 1: (SKP, yo) rep 3 times, SKP, k4.
Row 2 and all even rows: K.
Row 3: (SKP, yo) rep 3 times, SKP, k3.
Row 5: (SKP, yo) rep 3 times, SKP, k2.
Row 7: (SKP, yo) rep 3 times, SKP, k1
Row 9: K1, yo, (k2tog, yo) rep twice, k3.
Row 11: K1, yo, (k2tog, yo) rep twice, k4.
Row 13: K1, yo, (k2tog, yo) rep twice, k5.
Row 15: K1, yo, (k2tog, yo) rep twice, k6.
Rep rows 1–16 to continue the pattern.

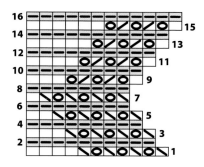

Beads

160 All Over in Garter Stitch

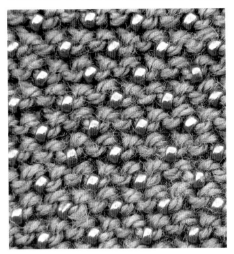

Pre-string any number of beads onto the yarn.
Begin with a multiple of 2 stitches.
Row 1: K.
Row 2: (K1, sld 1B, k1) rep across.
Repeat rows 1 and 2 to continue the pattern.

161 Scattered on Stockinette Stitch

Pre-string a multiple of 2 beads onto the yarn.
Begin with a multiple of 6 stitches, plus 1.
Row 1: (K4, p1, sld 1B, p1) rep to last st, k1.
Row 2 and all even rows: P.
Row 3: K1, (p1, sld 1B, p1, k4) rep across.
Repeat rows 1–4 to continue the pattern.

162 Checkered with Beads

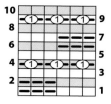

Pre-string a multiple of 6 beads onto the yarn.

Begin with a multiple of 6 stitches.

Row 1 and 2: (K3, p3) rep across.

Row 3 and 5: K.

Row 4: K1, (sld 1B, k2) rep to last st, sld 1B, k1.

Row 6 and 7: (P3, k3) rep across.

Row 8 and 10: P.

Row 9: P1, (sld 1B, p2) rep to last st, sld 1B, p1.

Repeat rows 1–10 to continue the pattern.

163 Vertical Stripes

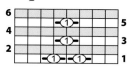

Pre-string a multiple of 4 beads onto the yarn.

Begin with a multiple of 8 stitches.

Row 1: K2, ((p1, sld 1B, p1) twice, k4) rep across,
ending with k2 instead of k4.

Row 2 and all even rows: P.

Row 3 and 5: K3, (p1, sld 1B, p1, k6) rep across, ending
with k3 instead of k6.

Repeat rows 1–6 to continue the pattern.

164 Small Clusters

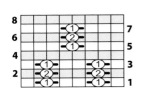

Pre-string a multiple of 12 beads onto the yarn.

Begin with a multiple of 8 stitches.

Row 1 and 3: K1, (p1, sld 1B, p1, k2) rep to last 3 sts, p1, sld 1B, p1, k1.

Row 2: P1, (k1, sld 2B, k1, p2) rep to last 3 sts, k1, sld 1B, k1, p1.

Row 4 and 8: P.

Row 5 and 7: K3, (p1, sld 1B, p1, k6) rep to last 5 sts, p1, sld 1B, p1, k3.

Row 6: P3, (k1, sld 2B, k1, p6) rep to last 5 sts, k1, sld 2B, k1, p3.

Repeat rows 1–8 to continue the pattern.

165 Large Clusters

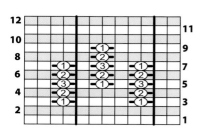

Pre-string a multiple of 18 beads, plus 9 beads onto the yarn.

Begin with a multiple of 8 stitches, plus 4.

Row 1: K.

Row 2: P.

Row 3: K2, (p1, sld 1B, p1, k4) rep to last 10 sts, p1, sld 1B, p1, k4, p1, sld 1B, p1, k2.

Row 4: P2, k1, sld 2B, k1, (p4, k1, sld 2B, k1) rep to last 2 sts, p2.

Row 5: K2, (p1, sld 3B, p1, k1, p1, sld 1B, p1, k1) rep to last 4 sts, p1, sld 3B, p1, k2.

Row 6: P2, k1, sld 2B, k1, (p1, k1, sld 2B, k1) rep to last 5 sts, p1, k1, sld 2B, k1, p2.

Row 7: K2, (p1, sld 1B, p1, k1, p1, sld 3B, p1, k1) rep to last 4 sts, p1, sld 1B, p1, k2.

Row 8: P5, (k1, sld 2B, k1, p4) rep to last 7 sts, k1, sld 2B, k1, p5.

Row 9: K5, (p1, sld 1B, p1, k4) rep to last 7 sts, p1, sld 1B, p1, k5.

Row 10: P.

Repeat rows 1–10 to continue the pattern.

166 ZigZag Clusters

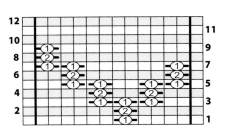

Pre-string a multiple of 24 beads onto the string.

Begin with a multiple of 12 stitches, plus 2.

Row 1: K5, (p1, sld 1B, p1, k10) rep across, ending with k7 instead of k10.

Row 2: P7, (k1, sld 2B, k1, p10) rep across, ending with p5 instead of p10.

Row 3: K3, (p1, (sld 1B, p2) twice, sld 1B, p1, k6) rep across, ending with k5 instead of k6.

Row 4: P5, (k1, sld 2B, p2, k1, sld 2B, p6) rep across ending with p3 instead of p6.

Row 5: K1, (p1, sld 1B, p2, sld 1B, p1, k2) rep across, ending with k3 instead of k2.

Row 6: P3, (k1, sld 2B, k1, p6, k1, sld 2B, k1, p2) rep across, ending with p1 instead of p2.

Row 7: K1, p1, sld 1B, p1, k6, (p1, sld 1B, (p2, sld 1B) twice, p1, k6) rep to last 5 sts, p1, sld 1B, p2, sld 1B, p1, k1.

Row 8: P1, (k1 sld 2B, k1, p10) rep across, ending with p11, instead of p10.

Row 9: K11, (p1, sld 1B, p1, k10) rep across, ending with k1 instead of k10.

Row 10 and 12: P.

Row 11: K.

BO.

167 Stripes and Diamonds

Pre-string a multiple of 48 beads onto the yarn.

Begin with a multiple of 12 stitches, plus 1.

Row 1: K3, ((k1, p1, sld 1B, p1) three times, k4) rep to last 9 sts, (p1, sld 1B, p1, k1) three times.

Row 2: P1, (k1, sld 1B, k1, p1, k1, sld 2B, k1, p1, k1, sld 1B, k1, p4) rep across.

Row 3: K3, ((k1, p1, sld 1B, p1, k1, p1, sld 3B, p1, k1, p1, sld 1B, p1, k4) rep to last 9 sts, p1, sld 1B, p1, k1, p1, sld 3B, p1, k1, p1, sld 1B, p1, k1.

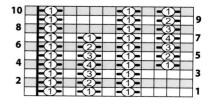

Row 4: P1, (k1, sld 1B, k1, p1, k1, sld 4B, k1, (p1, sld 1B, p1, k1) twice) rep across.

Row 5: K1, (p1, sld 2B, p1, k1, p1, sld 1B, p1, k1, p1, sld 3B, p1, k1, p1, sld 1B, k1) rep across.

Row 6: P1, (k1, sld 1B, k1, p1, k1, sld 2B, k1, p1, sld 1B, k1, p1, k1, p1, sld 3B, p1, k1) rep across.

Row 7: K1, (p1, sld 4B, p1, k1, (p1, sld 1B, p1, k1) three times) rep across.

Row 8: P1, (k1, sld 1B, k1, p4, k1, sld 1B, k1, p1, k1, sld 3B, k1, p1) rep across.

Row 9: K1, (p1, sld 2B, p1, k1, p1, sld 1B, p1, k4, p1, sld 1B, p1, k1) rep across.

Row 10: P1, (k1, sld 1B, k1, p4, (k1, sld 1B, k1, p1) twice) rep across.

Repeat rows 1–10 to continue the pattern.

168 Eyelets and Stripes

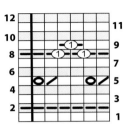

Pre-string a multiple of 3 beads onto the yarn.

Begin with a multiple of 6 stitches, plus 1.

Row 1, 2, 3, 7, and 11: K.

Row 4, 6, 10 and 12: P.

Row 5: K2tog, yo, (k2, k2tog, yo) rep to last st, k1.

Row 8: (K3, sld 1B, k2, sld 1B) rep to last 2 sts, k2.

Row 9: K2, (p1, sld 1B, p1, k4) rep across, ending with k3 instead of k4.

Repeat rows 1–10 to continue the pattern.

169 Lace and Beads

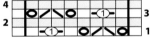

Pre-string a multiple of 2 beads onto the yarn.

Begin with a multiple of 8 stitches, plus 2.

Row 1: (K1, yo, SKP, k2tog, yo, k1, p1, sld 1B, p1) rep to last 2 sts, k2.

Row 2 and all even rows: P.

Row 3: K2, (p1, sld 1B, p1, k1, yo, SKP, k2tog, yo, k1) rep across.

Repeat rows 1–4 to continue the pattern.

170 Beads on a Vine

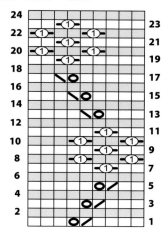

Pre-string a multiple of 14 beads onto the yarn.
Begin with a multiple of 8 stitches.
Row 1: K4, k2tog, yo, k3.
Row 2, 4, 6, 12, 14, 16, 18, 24: P.
Row 3: K3, k2tog, yo, k4.
Row 5: K2, k2tog, yo, k5.
Row 7, 9 and 11: K2, p1, sld 1B, p1, k5.
Row 8 and 10: P3, k1, sld 1B, k1, p2, k1, sld 1B, k1.
Row 13: K3, yo, SKP, k4.
Row 15: K4, yo, SKP, k3.
Row 17: K5, yo, SKP, k2.
Row 19, 21 and 23: K5, p1, sld 1B, p1, k2.
Row 20 and 22: K1, sld 1B, k1, p2, k1, sld 1B, k1, p3.
Repeat rows 1–24 to continue the pattern.

171 Beads and Ribbing

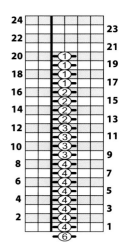

Pre-string a multiple of 62 beads onto the yarn.

Begin with a multiple of 4 stitches, plus 2.

With a simple CO, (CO 3 sts, slide 6 beads up to the needle) rep number times desired, CO 3 more sts.

Row 1, 3, 5 and 7: K2, (p1, sld 4B, p1, k2) rep across.

Row 2, 4, 6 and 8: P2, (k1, sld 4B, k1, p2) rep across.

Row 9 and 11: K2, (p1, sld 3B, p1, k2) rep across.

Row 10 and 12: P2, (k1, sld 3B, k1, p2) rep across.

Row 13 and 15: K2, (p1, sld 2B, p1, k2) rep across.

Row 14 and 16: P2, (k1, sld 2B, k1, p2) rep across.

Row 17 and 19: K2, (p1, sld 1B, p1, k2) rep across.

Row 18 and 20: P2, (k1, sld 1B, k1, p2) rep across.

Row 21 and 23: K.

Row 22: P.

Continue in St st to desired length.

172 Scalloped Edge

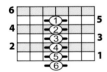

Pre-string a multiple of 21 beads onto the yarn.

Begin with a multiple of 6 stitches.

With a simple CO, (CO 3 sts, slide 6 beads up to the needle) rep number times desired, CO 3 more sts.

Row 1: K2, (p1, sld 5B, p1, k4) rep across, ending with k2 instead of k4.

Row 2: P2, (k1, sld 4B, k1, p4) rep across, ending with p2 instead of p4.

Row 3: K2, (p1, sld 3B, p1, k4) rep across, ending with k2 instead of k4.

Row 4: P2, (k1, sld 2B, k1, p4) rep across, ending with p2 instead of p4.

Row 5: K2, (p1, sld 1B, p1, k4) rep across, ending with k2 instead of k4.

Row 6: P.

Continue in St st to desired length.

173 Mini Scalloped Edge

Pre-string a multiple of 8 beads onto the yarn.

Begin with a multiple of 3 stitches, plus 1.

With a simple CO, (CO 2 sts, slide 3 beads up to the needle) rep number times desired, CO 2 more sts.

Row 1: K1, (p1, sld 2B, p1, k2) rep across, ending with k1 instead of k2.

Row 2 and 4: P1, (k1, sld 1B, k1, p2) rep across, ending with p1 instead of p2.

Row 3: K1, (p1, sld 1B, p1, k2) rep across, ending with k1 instead of k2.

Continue in St st to desired length.

174 Scallops and Diamonds

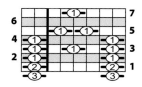

Pre-string a multiple of 12 beads, plus 8 beads onto the yarn.

Begin with a multiple of 6 stitches, plus 2.

With a simple CO, CO 1 st, slide 3 beads up to the needle, (CO 6 sts, slide 3 beads up to the needle) rep number times desired, CO one more st.

Row 1: P1, sld 2B, (p1, k4, p1, sld 2B, p1) rep across.

Row 2 and 4: K1, sld 1B, (k1, p4, k1, sld 1B, k1) rep across.

Row 3: P1, sld 1B, (p1, k1, p1, sld 1B, p1) rep across.

Row 5: K2, (p1, sld 1B, p2, sld 1B, k2) rep across.

Row 6: P.

Row 7: K3, (p1, sld 1B, p1, k4) rep across, ending with k3 instead of k4.

Continue in St st to desired length.

175 Triangle Edging

Pre-string a multiple of 10 beads onto the yarn.

Begin with a multiple of 13 stitches, plus 2.

Row 1: K.

Row 2 and all even rows: P.

Row 3: K2, (p1, sld 1B, p1, k1, (p1, sld 1B, p1) rep 4 times, k2) rep across.

Row 5: K6, ((p1, sld 1B, p1) rep 3 times, k7) rep to last 9 sts, ((p1, sld 1B, p1) rep 3 times, k3.

Row 7 and 9: K8, (p1, sld 1B, p1, k11) rep to last 7 sts, p1, sld 1B, p1, k5.

Row 11: K.

Continue in St st to desired length.

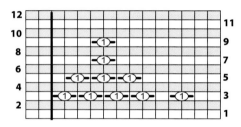

176 Bead Knitted Diamonds

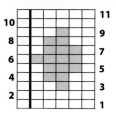

Pre-string a multiple of 16 beads onto the yarn.

Begin with a multiple of 5 stitches, plus 1.

On all right side rows, knit into the back of the stitch
  wrapping the yarn over the right needle, clockwise.

Row 1 and 11: K.

Row 2 and 10: P.

Row 3 and 9: K2, (kB1, k4) rep to last st, k1.

Row 4 and 8: P2, (pB2, p3) rep across, ending with p2
  instead of p3.

Row 5 and 7: K1, (kB3, k2) rep across.

Row 6: (P1, pB4) rep to last st, p1.

BO.

177 Bead Knitted Sprig

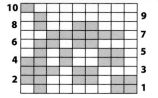

Pre-string 38 beads onto the yarn.

Motif is 9 stitches.

On all right side rows, knit into the back of the stitch
  wrapping the yarn over the right needle, clockwise.

Row 1: KB2, k5, kB1, k1.

Row 2: PB2, p2, pB2, p1, pB2.

Row 3: K3, kB2, k1, kB3.

Row 4: PB2, p1, pB1, p2, pB2, p1.

Row 5: K1, kB2, k2, kB1, k1, kB1, k1.

Row 6: P1, pB2, p1, pB2, p3.

Row 7: K1, kB6, k2.

Row 8: P1, pB1, p2, pB2, p3.

Row 9: K7, kB1, k1.

Row 10: PB1, p8.

BO.

178 Bead Knitted Branch

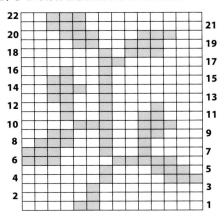

Pre-string 83 beads onto the yarn.

Begin with a multiple of 14 stitches.

On all right side rows, knit into the back of the stitch, wrapping the yarn over the right needle, clockwise.

Row 1: K8, B2, k4.

Row 2: P5, B1, p8.

Row 3: K8, B1, k5.

Row 4: P6, B1, p4, B3.

Row 5: K1, B3, k3, b1, k6.

Row 6: B3, p4, B5, p2.

Row 7: K4, B1, k2, B1, k3, B3.

Row 8: P1, B3, (p2, B1) twice, p4.

Row 9: K3, B2, k2, B1, k2, B2, k2.

Row 10: P4, B3, p2, B3, p2.

Row 11: K3, B2, (k2, B1) twice, k3.

Row 12: P3, B1, p2, (B1, p3) twice.

Row 13: K7, B1, k2, B2, k2.

Row 14: P2, B3, p1, B1, p7.

Row 15: K7, B1, k2, B2, k2.

Row 16: P3, B1, p2, B1, p7.

Row 17: K6, B2, k6.

Row 18: P6, B1, p1, B3, p3.

Row 19: K3, B3, k2, B2, k4.

Row 20: (P3, B3) twice, p2.

Row 21: K9, B3, k2.

Row 22: P2, B3, p9.

BO.

179 Bead Knitted Fan

Pre-string 112 beads onto the yarn.

Begin with 18 stitches.

On all right side rows, knit into the back of the stitch wrapping the yarn over the right needle, clockwise.

Row 1 and 28: K.Row 2 and 27: P.

Row 3: K8, B2, k8.

Row 4: P7, B3, p8.

Row 5: K7, B4, k7.

Row 6: P6, B1, (p1, B1) twice, p7.

Row 7: K6, B1, k1, B2, k1, B1, k6.

Row 8: P5, (B1, p2) twice, B1, p6.

Row 9: K5, B1, k2, B2, k2, B1, k5.

Row 10: P4, B1, p2, B3, p2, B1, p5.

Row 11: K4, B1, k2, B4, k2, B1, k4.

Row 12: P3, B1, p2, B1, (p1, B1) twice, p2, B1, p4.

Row 13: K3, B1, k2, B1, k1, B2, k1, B1, k2, B1, k3.

Row 14: (P2, B1) rep 5 times, p3.

Row 15: (K2, B1) twice, k2, B2, (K2, B1) twice, k2.

Row 16: P1, B1, p2, B1, p2, B3, (p2, B1) twice, p2.

Row 17: K1, (B1, k2) twice, B4, (k2, B1) twice, k1.

Row 18: P3, B1, p2, (B1, p1) twice, B1, p2, B1, p4.

Row 19: K3, B1, k2, B1, k1, B2, k1, B1, k2, B1, k3

Row 20: (P2, B1) rep 5 times, p3.

Row 21: K5, B1, k2, B2, k2, B1, k5.

Row 22: P4, B1, p2, B3, p2, B1, p5.

Row 23: K4, B1, k2, B4, k2, B1, k4.

Row 24: P6, B1, (p1, B1) twice, p7.

Row 25: K6, B1, k1, B2, k1, B1, k6.

Row 26: P8, B1, p9.

BO.

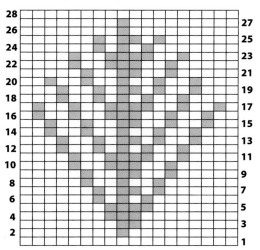

184 ～

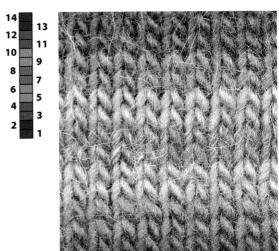

Colorwork
Stripes

180 Basic Two Row Stripe

181 Mirror Stripe Twos

182 Mirror Stripe Ones

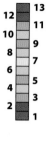

183 Mirror Stripes Uneven

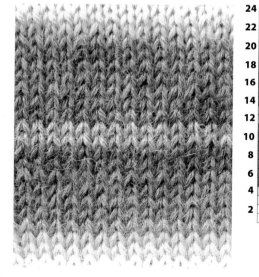

184 Uneven Stripe

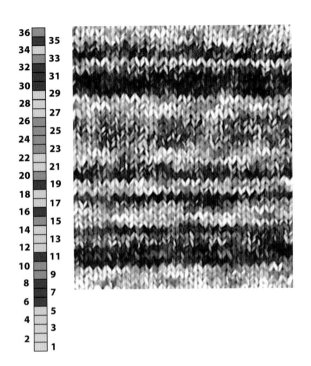

Slip Stitch

A reminder about Slip Stitch charts: The slip stitch charts begin with a bar across the bottom. This shows the color yarn to use for casting on. The boxes on either side of the chart show which color is used to knit that row. (See Slip Stitch in Basics section on page 55.)

185 Heel Stitch

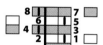

186 Stripe

187 Two-Way Stripes

188 Textured Stripe

189 Stripes and Shadows

190 Stairs

191 Slanting Steps

192 Wave

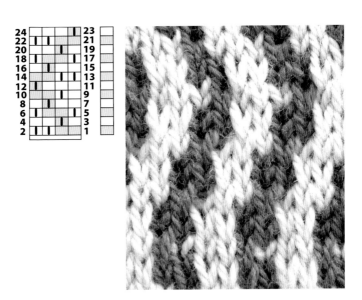

193 Railroad

194 Hills and Valleys

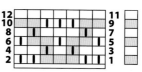

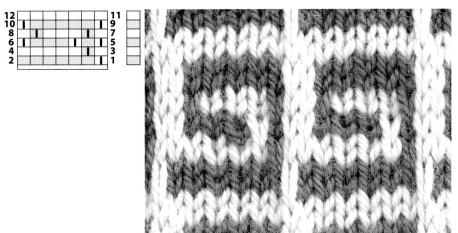

195 Mini Maze

196 Double Maze

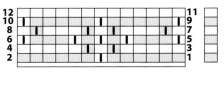

Intarsia

(See *Intarsia* in the Basics section on page 57.)

197 Diagonal Split

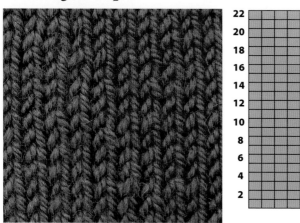
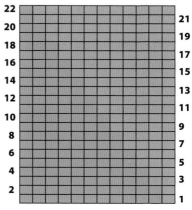

198 Squares

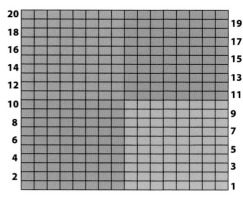

199 Dot

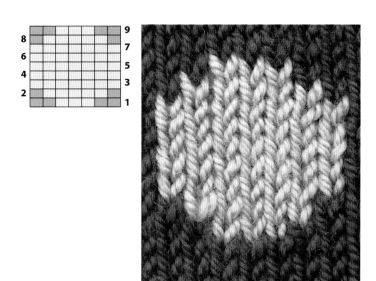

200 Heart

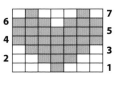

201 Argyle

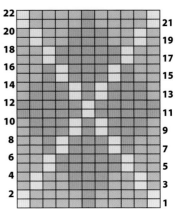

Stranding

202 All Over

203 Dotted

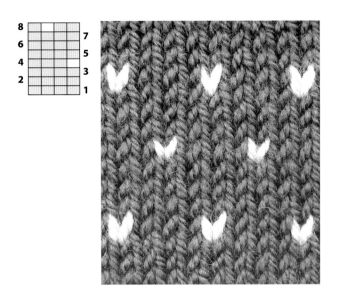

204 V's in a Row

205 Scattered V's

206 Stepped Strip

207 Bordered ZigZag

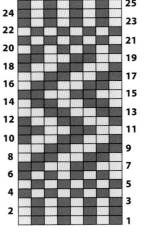

208 Hound's Tooth

209 Diamonds

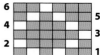

210 Mini Diamonds

211 Stripes and Diagonals

212 Slanting Diamonds

213 Squares and Diamonds

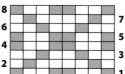

214 Marching Triangles

215 Star

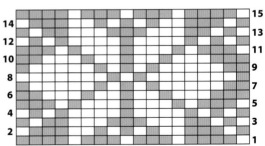

216 Garden Blooms

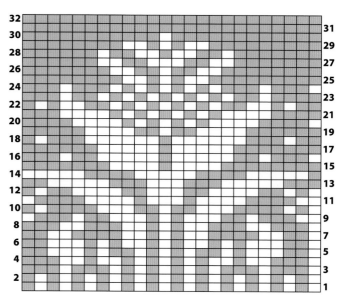

Section 3: Basic Projects

A scarf, a hat, a sweater, gloves and socks, these are the basic projects that just about every knitter will want to know how to make at some point in his or her knitting experience. This section has all of these in basic forms, as well as several variations that touch on some of the many design possibilities. The basic patterns are meant to be used again and again, to create any number of different designs. Beginning with the basic patterns, it is easy to add a little detail, by choosing a stitch pattern from Section 2 to make your project special. Whether making your first project such as the basic rolled edge hat, or looking for a more complex pattern, such as the Sampler Sweater, you will have a ready reference of projects for you to knit.

Shawls and Scarves

Simple rectangles and triangles are great starting points for all levels of knitters. Without worries of shape or fit, beginners can practice knitting techniques with basic stitches, while advanced knitters can work on intricate patterns, or delicate yarns, creating fabulous pieces of hand knitting. Large needles and beautifully textured yarn work up into fast gifts of easy-to-knit scarves in garter stitch.

Triangle Shawl

This thick and cozy shawl is easy to make with a simple increase, made by knitting or purling into the front and the back of the first stitch in each row. Because the variegated yarns contain some of the same colors, the color pattern you create is subtle from close up, almost blending together, but then when you stand back you can see the changing stripes. If you don't want to bother with working the border edging, which can be cumbersome with the three long double pointed needles, you can just continue with the increases at the edge, working in the color pattern until the shawl is as large as you choose.

Skill level worked with the border

INTERMEDIATE

Skill level worked without the border

BEGINNER

Finished measurements

60" wide by 40" from center top to bottom point

Materials list

Ten 55 yd. skeins of bulky weight variegated yarn, 4 light, 3 medium, 3 dark.

Size 13 needles, 3 pair 32" circular (you will only need one pair if you are making the shawl without a border.)

Stitch markers

Gauge

In stockinette stitch, 9½ sts and 13 rows = 4".

Yarn used for samples shown

Lion Brand Yarn's Landscapes
(50% wool/50% acrylic, 55 yd., 1.75 oz.), colors: 4 skeins of #273 Spring Desert, 3 skeins each of #277 Country Sunset and #279 Deep Sea.

Notes

To increase at the beginning of the knit row, knit into the front and the back of the first stitch.
To increase at the beginning of the purl row, purl into the front and the back of the first stitch.

Repeat color sequence three times from bottom to top.

Instructions

Beg with the dark yarn, CO 1 st.
Row 1: Inc - 2 sts.
Row 2: Inc, p1 - 3 sts.
Row 3: Inc, k2 - 4 sts.
Row 4: Inc, p3 - 5 sts.
Row 5: Inc, k4 - 6 sts.
Row 6: Inc, p5 - 7 sts.
Row 7: Inc, k6 - 8 sts.
Row 8: Inc, p7 - 9 sts.
Row 9: Inc, k8 - 10 sts.
Row 10: Inc, p9 - 11 sts.

Continue increasing one st at the beg of ea row while working the following color pattern 3 times:

3 light
1 medium
1 dark
2 light
1 dark
1 medium
2 light
4 medium
3 light
3 dark
1 medium
1 light
1 dark
1 medium
5 light
3 dark
2 medium
1 dark

Do not bind off.

Border

Using the other two circular needles and the light colored yarn, pick up 102 sts along ea of the sides, placing stitch markers at each of the three corners before the center stitch. Working in the round with the light colored yarn, knit 7 rounds, increasing one stitch in the stitch before and after each corner stitch. Change to the dark yarn and knit one round with no increases. Purl one round. BO, weave in ends.

Lace Sampler Shawl

This shawl is a great way to try out several lace patterns and colors of yarn to see if you like knitting them and to see how they look next to each other. By using a variety of patterns, the finished shawl is much more interesting than a lace shawl worked in a single repeat. It is easy to make your own design of your favorite lace patterns by just lining up several repeats and working them into a large strip of knitting. To make a gradual change from one skein to the next when using different colored skeins, as I did, when you have worked almost all the yarn of the first skein, you can gradually change to the color of the new skein by switching skeins of yarn every few rows, then every row, then every few rows again, then working only with the new color. Finally, blocking is the key to making your lace look light and airy. The further you stretch your lace when blocking, the lacier effect you will achieve.

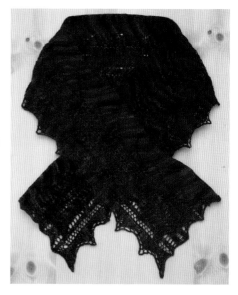

Skill level

INTERMEDIATE

Finished measurements

22" wide by 60" with two skeins of yarn, or 90" with three

Materials list

SUPER FINE

3 different colors (A, B, C) of 55 yd. skeins of lace weight variegated yarn.

Size 6 needles (14" long or circulars)

Stitch markers

For blocking: Straight pins, clean white sheet, large carpeted area to pin finished piece.

Gauge

In stockinette stitch stretched for lace, 16 sts and 24 rows = 4"

Yarn used for samples shown

Mountain Colors Bearfoot (60% super-wash wool/25% mohair/15% nylon, 350 yd., 3.5 oz.), colors: one skein each of Wildflower (A), Crazy Woman (B), and Winter Sky (C).

Notes

You don't have to use stitch markers, but it helps to know when each pattern repeat begins and ends so you can keep track of your patterns and catch any errors right away.

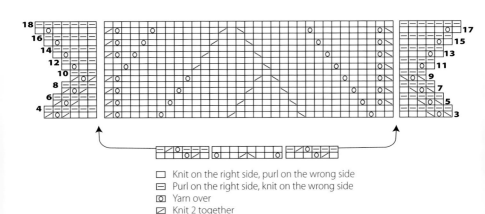

☐ Knit on the right side, purl on the wrong side
⊟ Purl on the right side, knit on the wrong side
☒ Yarn over
☑ Knit 2 together
☒ Skp

Instructions

Using A, CO 87 sts.

Row 1 and 2: Knit.

Row 3: Following the chart or line by line instructions, work row 3, placing stitch markers between each pattern sequence. Work through row 18, then repeat rows 3–18 until you have about 16 yards of yarn left. Continuing in patt, work one row in B, two rows in A, one row in B, two rows in A. Work one row in B, one row in A, one row in B, one row in A. Work two rows in B, one row in A, two rows in B, one row in A. Continue with B until you have about 8 yards left. Repeat the same color change from color B to C as you did for color A to B. Continue with C until you have about 3 yards left. Knit two rows, BO loosely. Weave in ends.

Line by line instructions:

Row 3: K2togtb, yo, k2togtb, k3, pm, k1, k2tog, yo, k3, yo, k2, k2togtb, k2tog, k2, yo, k1, k2tog, yo, k3, pm, k2, yo, k7, k2togtb, k7, k2tog, k7, yo, k4, yo, k2tog, pm, k1, k2tog, yo, k3, yo, k2, k2togtb, k2tog, k2, yo, k1, k2tog, yo, k3, pm, k3, k2tog, yo, k2tog - 85 sts.

Row 4: K6, (m), k1, k2tog, yo, k3, p8, k1, k2tog, yo, k3, (m), p33, (m), k1, k2tog, yo, k3, p8, k1, k2tog, yo, k3, (m), k6.

Row 5: K2togtb, yo, k2togtb, k2, (m), k1, k2tog, yo, k3, yo, k2, k2togtb, k2tog, k2, yo, k1, k2tog, yo, k3, (m), k2togtb, yo, k1, yo, k7, k2togtb, k5, k2tog, k7, yo, k5, yo, k2tog, (m), k1, k2tog, yo, k3, yo, k2, k2togtb, k2tog, k2, yo, k1, k2tog, yo, k3, (m), k2, k2tog, yo, k2tog - 83 sts.

Row 6: K5, (m), k1, k2tog, yo, k3, p8, k1, k2tog, yo, k3, (m), p33, (m), k1, k2tog, yo, k3, p8, k1, k2tog, yo, k3, (m), k5.

Row 7: K2togtb, yo, k2togtb, k1, (m), k1, k2tog, yo, k3, yo, k2, k2togtb, k2tog, k2, yo, k1, k2tog, yo, k3, (m), k2togtb, yo, k2, yo, k7, k2togtb, k3, k2tog, k7, yo, k6, yo, k2tog, (m), k1, k2tog, yo, k3, yo, k2, k2togtb, k2tog, k2, yo, k1, k2tog, yo, k3, (m), k1, k2tog, yo, k2tog - 81 sts.

Row 8: K4, (m), k1, k2tog, yo, k3, p8, k1, k2tog, yo, k3, (m), p33, (m), k1, k2tog, yo, k3, p8, k1, k2tog, yo, k3, (m), k4.

Row 9: K2togtb, yo, k2togtb, (m), k1, k2tog, yo, k3, yo, k2, k2togtb, k2tog, k2, yo, k1, k2tog, yo, k3, (m), k2togtb, yo, k3, yo, k7, k2togtb, k1, k2tog, k7, yo, k7, yo, k2tog, (m), k1, k2tog, yo, k3, yo, k2, k2togtb, k2tog, k2, yo, k1, k2tog, yo, k3, (m), k2tog, yo, k2tog - 79 sts.

Row 10: K3, (m), k1, k2tog, yo, k3, p8, k1, k2tog, yo, k3, (m), p33, (m), k1, k2tog, yo, k3, p8, k1, k2tog, yo, k3, (m), k3.

Row 11: K1, yo, k2, (m), k1, k2tog, yo, k3, yo, k2, k2togtb, k2tog, k2, yo, k1, k2tog, yo, k3, (m), k2togtb, yo, k4, yo, k7, k2togtb, k7, k2tog, k7, yo, k2, (m), k1, k2tog, yo, k3, yo, k2, k2togtb, k2tog, k2, yo, k1, k2tog, yo, k3, (m), k2, yo, k1 - 81 sts.

Row 12: K4, (m), k1, k2tog, yo, k3, p8, k1, k2tog, yo, k3, (m), p33, (m), k1, k2tog, yo, k3, p8, k1, k2tog, yo, k3, (m), k4.

Row 13: K1, yo, k3, (m), k1, k2tog, yo, k3, yo, k2, k2togtb, k2tog, k2, yo, k1, k2tog, yo, k3, (m), k2togtb, yo, k5, yo, k7, k2togtb, k5, k2tog, k7, yo, k1, yo, k2tog, (m), k1, k2tog, yo, k3, yo, k2, k2togtb, k2tog, k2, yo, k1, k2tog, yo, k3, (m), k3, yo, k1 - 83 sts.

Row 14: K5, (m), k1, k2tog, yo, k3, p8, k1, k2tog, yo, k3, (m), p33, (m), k1, k2tog, yo, k3, p8, k1, k2tog, yo, k3, (m), k5.

Row 15: K1, yo, k4, (m), k1, k2tog, yo, k3, yo, k2, k2togtb, k2tog, k2, yo, k1, k2tog, yo, k3, (m), k2togtb, yo, k6, yo, k7, k2togtb, k3, k2tog, k7, yo, k2, yo, k2tog, (m), k1, k2tog, yo, k3, yo, k2, k2togtb, k2tog, k2, yo, k1, k2tog, yo, k3, (m), k4, yo, k1 - 85 sts.

Row 16: K6, (m), k1, k2tog, yo, k3, p8, k1, k2tog, yo, k3, (m), p33, (m), k1, k2tog, yo, k3, p8, k1, k2tog, yo, k3, (m), k6.

Row 17: K1, yo, k5, (m), k1, k2tog, yo, k3, yo, k2, k2togtb, k2tog, k2, yo, k1, k2tog, yo, k3, (m), k2togtb, yo, k7, yo, k7, k2togtb, k1, k2tog, k7, yo, k3, yo, k2tog, (m), k1, k2tog, yo, k3, yo, k2, k2togtb, k2tog, k2, yo, k1, k2tog, yo, k3, (m), k5, yo, k1 - 87 sts.

Row 18: K7, (m), k1, k2tog, yo, k3, p8, k1, k2tog, yo, k3, (m), p33, (m), k1, k2tog, yo, k3, p8, k1, k2tog, yo, k3, (m), k7.

Blocking

Using warm water, dampen the knitting. Roll in a clean dry towel to remove excess moisture. Stretch the shawl across a large flat surface, such as carpeting covered with a clean sheet, pinning the scarf at each point along the sides and shaping the ends. Continue stretching the knitting and straightening it so it is even and approximately the finished dimensions. Let dry, then remove pins.

Hats

Once you are ready to move beyond basic scarves, hats are one of the best beginner projects in knitting. When making a hat, you acquire new, important skills, such as knitting in the round, or sewing a seam, as well as planning a finished hat that will fit on someone's head. Gauge becomes important, and you learn to understand a pattern and alter it, if necessary.

Basic Rolled Edge Hat

This basic hat and two variations will fit most adults. You may want to adjust the patterns for someone with a larger or smaller head size. The trick to getting a hat to fit well is to get the correct measurement for the hat around the head, as well as the length from the center of the hat to the bottom of the brim. If you can, it is best to measure the hat recipient before beginning. Then, since a hat should fit snuggly, you will need to subtract about 1" from the measurement around the head before calculating your gauge. It may take some trial and error before you get the best fitting hat for an unusual head size.

Skill level

EASY

Finished Size

Basic Rolled Edge and Simple Rib Variation to fit size 21" to 23" head circumference.

Cable Rib Variation to fit size 20" to 22" head circumference.

Materials list

One 4 oz. ball of worsted weight yarn

Size 8, 20" circular needles (for cast on and ribbing)

Size 8, double pointed needles for crown of hat

Tapestry needle

Stitch markers

Gauge

In stockinette stitch, 16 sts and 22 rows = 4"

Yarn used for samples shown

Lorna's Laces Bullfrogs and Butterflies (85% wool/15% mohair, 4 oz., 190 yd.)
Basic Rolled Edge Hat: one skein in Icehouse

Ribbed Variation: one skein in Lakeview

Cable Variation: one skein in Berry

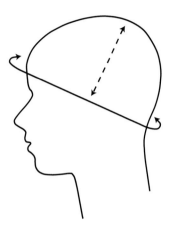

Two measurements are needed for a well fitting hat.

Instructions

Brim

CO 80 sts, join into a circle, pm. Work in St st for 5½". End at marker, use marker as first "pm" in Crown section.

Crown

(Pm, k2tog, k8) rep around - 70 sts.

*K 1 rnd with no decreases.
(K2tog, k to marker) rep around - 10 sts decreased.

Rep from * until 16 sts remain. Cut yarn to 6", pass through rem sts, weave in ends.

Ribbed Variation

The ribbing on this hat helps to pull the hat in tighter so you work with more stitches on the needle than the plain rolled edge hat.

Skill level

EASY

Instructions

CO 88 sts, join into a circle, pm. Work in k2, p2 rib for 6". Work in stockinette stitch for 2". End at marker, use marker as first "pm" in Crown section.

Crown

(Pm, k2tog, k9) rep around - 80 sts.

*K 1 rnd with no decreases.
(K2tog, k to marker) rep around - 8 sts decreased.

Rep from asterisk until 16 sts remain. Cut yarn to 6", pass through rem sts, weave in ends.

Cable Variation, Worked Flat

The cable ribbing on this hat pulls in even more than the simple ribbed variation hat above. This hat is a little tighter fit than the other two hats.

Skill level

EASY

Instructions

Brim

Using the same yarn, needles and gauge, CO 90 sts.
Following the chart or the line-by-line instructions below, work the cable repeat for 6".
Work in St st for 2". Dec 2 sts on the next right side row   88 sts.

Crown

*Purl next row. (K2tog, k13, pm) rep across, omit placing marker after last st. Rep from asterisk until 18 sts remain. Cut yarn to 18", pass through rem sts, sew seam, weave in ends.

Cable Repeat line by line instructions:

Row 1: P1, (2 sts to cn in back, k2, k sts from cn, p2, k4, p2) rep across, ending with p1 instead of p2.

Row 2 and all even rows: K1, (p4, k2, p2, k2) rep across, ending with k1 instead of k2.

Row 3 and 5: P1, (k2, p2, 2 sts to cn in back, k2, k sts from cn, 2 sts to cn in front, k2, k sts from cn, p2) rep across, ending with p1 instead of p2.

Sweaters

A sweater project combines a variety of knitting techniques and skills that all need to come together in order to complete your project successfully. Like a large shawl or blanket, a sweater is an investment in time and materials. In addition to being a larger project, knitting a sweater includes shaping, assembling finished knitted pieces and most importantly, fitting the project to a wearer. It is very rewarding to complete a well-made and well-fitting sweater, all of which takes planning and attention to detail. Once you have made a sweater or two, you will have knitting confidence to tackle any project you desire.

The instructions for knitting any outfit are general for an average range of sizes. They are seldom the actual measurements in all places for individuals. That is why it helps a great deal to check the finished measurements against a similar outfit that fits you well. Then you will know if you need to lengthen a sleeve or make it wider at the armhole so that it will fit you the way you like your clothes. Take measurements for the width and length of all the pieces, then adjust the pattern before beginning. You may just need to knit the body and sleeves a little longer to make the perfect sweater for you. It's also a good idea to make a note of the changes you made and for whom the finished item was for, so if you decide to make something similar for the same person, you will already have the dimensions.

Basic Dropped Shoulder Sweater

This unisex sweater is one of the easiest large projects you can make. Other than a little bit of shaping at the neckline, and increasing for the sleeves, there is nothing else that's difficult. The simple shapes make this a fantastic project for having fun with patterns and textures. If you make it big and loose, it will be the most comfortable sweater in your wardrobe. It's also a great project to make as a gift, because you don't have to worry about fit as much as for closer fitting garments.

Skill level

EASY

Sizes
To fit chest sizes
34 (36, 38, 40, 42, 44, 46)"

Knitted Measurements
Chest 38 (40, 42, 44, 46, 48, 50)"
Length 23 (23½, 23½, 24, 24, 25, 25)"
Upper Arm 18 (19, 19, 20, 20, 21, 21)"

MEDIUM

Materials list
Six 4 oz. balls of worsted weight yarn
Size 8, 26" and 20" circular needles
Tapestry needle
Stitch markers

Gauge
In stockinette stitch
18 sts and 24 rows = 4"

Yarn used for samples shown
Basic Solid Colored Sweater: Brown Sheep's Lamb's Pride (85% wool/15% mohair, 4 oz., 190 yd.) six skeins of color #M29 Jack's Plum.

Basic Striped Sweater: Brown Sheep's Lamb's Pride (85% wool/15% mohair, 4 oz., 190 yd.), two skeins of #M185 Abergine; two skeins of #M29 Jack's Plum; one skein each of #M175 Bronze Patina; #M181 Prairie Fire; #M05 Onyx; #M89 Roasted Coffee.

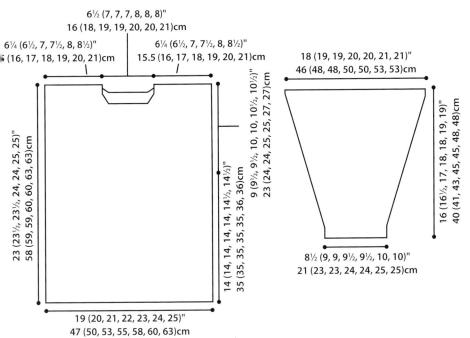

Back and schematic measurements:

6½ (7, 7, 7, 8, 8, 8)"
16 (18, 19, 19, 20, 20, 21)cm

6¼ (6½, 7, 7½, 8, 8½)"
[1]6 (16, 17, 18, 19, 20, 21)cm

6¼ (6½, 7, 7½, 8, 8½)"
15.5 (16, 17, 18, 19, 20, 21)cm

18 (19, 19, 20, 20, 21, 21)"
46 (48, 48, 50, 50, 53, 53)cm

9 (9½, 9½, 10, 10, 10½, 10½)"
23 (24, 24, 25, 25, 27, 27)cm

23 (23½, 23½, 24, 24, 25, 25)"
58 (59, 59, 60, 60, 63, 63)cm

14 (14, 14, 14, 14, 14½, 14½)"
35 (35, 35, 35, 35, 36, 36)cm

16 (16½, 17, 18, 18, 19, 19)"
40 (41, 43, 45, 45, 48, 48)cm

8½ (9, 9, 9½, 9½, 10, 10)"
21 (23, 23, 24, 24, 25, 25)cm

19 (20, 21, 22, 23, 24, 25)"
47 (50, 53, 55, 58, 60, 63)cm

Back

CO 84 (88, 94, 98, 104, 108, 112) sts.
Work in St st until piece meas ¾" less than finished length.

Shape Neckline

On next right side row k 28 (29, 32, 34, 34, 36, 38) sts, transfer center 28 (30, 30, 30, 36, 36, 36) sts to st holder, attach new ball of yarn and k rem 28 (29, 32, 34, 34, 36, 38) sts.
Work ea side separately.
Dec 1 st on neck edge on next two rows - 26 (27, 30, 32, 32, 34, 36) sts.
Work 2 more rows even in St st.
BO.

Front

Work the same as for the back until piece meas 3 (3.5, 3.5, 3.5, 3.5, 4, 4)" less than finished length.

Shape Neckline:

On next right side row, k33 (34, 37, 39, 39, 41, 43) sts, transfer center 18 (20, 20, 20, 26, 26, 26) sts to st holder, attach new ball of yarn and k rem 33 (34, 37, 39, 39, 41, 43) sts.
Work ea side separately.
Dec 1 st on neck edge on next 7 rows - 26 (27, 30, 32, 32, 34, 36) sts.
Work 10 (14, 14, 14, 14, 17, 17) more rows even in St st.
BO.

Sleeves (make two)

CO 38 (40, 40, 42, 42, 44, 44) sts.
Work the same as for back through row 14, increasing 1 st ea side on row 14 - 40 (42, 42, 44, 44, 46, 46) sts.
Continuing in St st, inc 1 st ea end every fourth row 21 (22, 22, 23, 23, 24, 24) times - 82 (86, 86, 90, 90, 94, 94) sts. Work even in St st until sleeve meas finished length.
BO.

Assembly and Finishing

Sew the front to back at shoulders.

Collar: With the right side of knitting facing you, pick up and knit 3 sts from the right back neck edge, 28 (30, 30, 30, 36, 36, 36) sts from the back st holder, 3 sts from the left back neck edge, 14 (18, 18, 18, 18, 21, 21) sts from left front neck edge, 18 (20, 20, 20, 26, 26, 26) sts from the front st holder, and 14 (18, 18, 18, 18, 21, 21) sts from right front neck edge 80 (92, 92, 92, 104, 110, 110) sts.
Knit in the round for 3".
BO loosely.

Sleeves and Side seams: Center the sleeves over the shoulder seams and sew to the sides of the front and back. Sew the sleeve and front and back side seams tog.

Striped Variation

Working a simple pattern in bold stripes with a decorative edge is a great way to enhance a basic design. You can use the colors I've worked this piece in, or create your own color pattern, using your favorite colors.

Skill level

EASY

For All Pieces

Beginning with the burgundy yarn, CO the same number of sts needed for your size in the Basic Dropped Shoulder Sweater.
Row 1–3: K.
Row 4: (K1, p1) rep across.
Row 5 and 6: (P1, k1) rep across.
Row 7 and 8: (K1, p1) rep across.
Row 9: (P1, k1) rep across.
Row 10–14: P.
Continue with the burgundy for 4 rows in St st, then rep the above color sequence for the rest of the pieces, working all shaping for neck and sleeve increases the same as the Basic Dropped Sweater instructions.

Basic Set-in Sleeve Sweater

For a closer fitting garment that conforms more to the shape of the body, here is a sweater with set in sleeves. The sleeves and body require more shaping and care in assembly, but the resulting sweater results in a closer fitting garment, with less bulk at the armholes. This style is made with simple rolled edges, but you could easily begin with a ribbing along the lower edge and sleeves instead. The yarn can be a simple solid, or a self striping yarn, leaving you to enjoy knitting in stockinette stitch throughout the piece.

Skill level

INTERMEDIATE

Sizes
To fit chest sizes
34 (36, 38, 40, 42, 44, 46)"

Knitted Measurements
Chest 38 (40, 42, 45, 47, 49, 51)"
Length 21.5 (22, 22.5, 22.5, 23, 23.5, 23.5)"
Upper Arm 12.5 (13, 13.5, 14, 14.5, 15, 15)"

MEDIUM

Materials list
Six 4 oz. balls of worsted weight yarn

Size 7, 26" and 20" circular needles

Tapestry needle

Stitch markers

Gauge
In stockinette stitch
18 sts and 24 rows = 4"

Yarn used for samples shown
Basic Solid Colored Sweater: Brown Sheep's Cotton Fleece (80% cotton/20% merino wool, 3.5 oz., 215 yd.) six skeins in color CW-820 Teddy Bear.

Sampler Tunic: Louet Gems (100% merino wool, 1.5 oz., 175 yd.) 6 skeins in color Champagne.

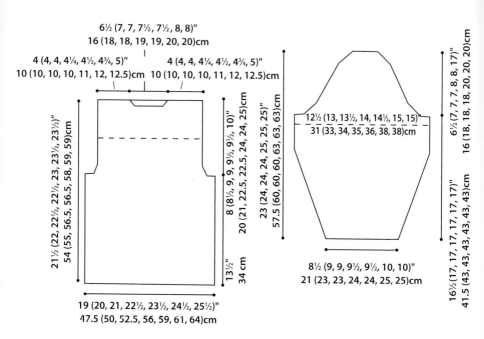

6½ (7, 7, 7½, 7½, 8, 8)"
16 (18, 18, 19, 19, 20, 20)cm

4 (4, 4, 4¼, 4½, 4¾, 5)"
10 (10, 10, 10, 11, 12, 12.5)cm 10 (10, 10, 10, 11, 12, 12.5)cm

4 (4, 4, 4¼, 4½, 4¾, 5)"

21½ (22, 22½, 22½, 23, 23½, 23½)"
54 (55, 56.5, 56.5, 58, 59, 59)cm

8 (8½, 9, 9, 9½, 9½, 10)"
20 (21, 22.5, 22.5, 24, 24, 25)cm

23 (24, 24, 24, 25, 25, 25)"
57.5 (60, 60, 60, 63, 63, 63)cm

13½"
34 cm

19 (20, 21, 22½, 23½, 24½, 25½)"
47.5 (50, 52.5, 56, 59, 61, 64)cm

12½ (13, 13½, 14, 14½, 15, 15)"
31 (33, 34, 35, 36, 38, 38)cm

6½ (7, 7, 7, 8, 8, 17)"
16 (18, 18, 18, 20, 20, 20)cm

16½ (17, 17, 17, 17, 17, 17)"
41.5 (43, 43, 43, 43, 43, 43)cm

8½ (9, 9, 9½, 9½, 10, 10)"
21 (23, 23, 24, 24, 25, 25)cm

Back

CO 84 (86, 90, 94, 100, 104, 108) sts.

Knit in St st until piece is 12 (12.5, 13, 13.5 14, 14.5, 15)" long from cast on (includes extra 1" for rolled edge).

Armhole Shaping:

BO 4 (4, 5, 6, 6, 6, 7) sts at beg of next 2 rows - 76 (78, 80, 82, 88, 92, 94) sts.

Dec 1 st every RS row 6 (6, 6, 6, 7, 7, 7) times - 64 (66, 68, 70, 74, 78, 80) sts.

Work even until armhole meas 7.5 (8, 8.5, 9, 9, 9.5, 9.5)".

Shape Neckline

On next right side row k 21 (21, 21, 21, 22, 23, 24) sts, transfer center 22 (24, 26, 28, 30, 32, 32) sts to st holder, attach new ball of yarn and k rem 21 (21, 21, 21, 22, 23, 24) sts.

Work ea side separately.

Dec 1 st at center on next 3 rows. At the same time, BO 6 (6, 6, 6, 7, 7, 8) sts at shoulder on next two rows that begin at the shoulder.

BO rem 6 (6, 6, 6, 8, 8, 8) sts.

Work 2 more rows even in St st.

BO.

Front

Work the same as for the back until piece meas 4" less than finished length.

Shape Neckline:

On next right side row, k24 (24, 24, 25, 26, 27) sts, transfer center 16 (18, 20, 22, 24, 26, 26) sts to st holder, attach new ball of yarn and k rem 24 (24, 24, 25, 26, 27) sts.

Work ea side separately.

Dec 1 st on neck edge on next 6 rows - 18 (18, 18, 18, 19, 20, 21) sts.

Work 16 more rows even in St st.

BO 6 (6, 6, 6, 7, 7, 8) sts at shoulder on next 2 rows that begin at shoulder edge.

BO rem 6 (6, 6, 6, 8, 8, 8) sts.

Sleeves (make two)

CO 40 (40, 42, 42, 44, 44, 46) sts.

Every 13th (12th, 12th, 11th, 10th, 9th, 9th) row inc 1 st ea side 7 (8, 8, 9, 10, 11, 11) times - 54 (56, 58, 60, 64, 66, 68) sts and 91 (96, 96, 99, 100, 99, 99) rows.

Work 3 (0, 2, 3, 2, 6, 6) more rows.

BO 4 (4, 5, 5, 6, 6, 6) sts at beg of next 2 rows - 46 (48, 48, 50, 52, 54, 56) sts.

Dec 1 st ea end every RS row 5 (6, 6, 7, 7, 7, 8) times, then every 3rd row 5 times, then every RS row 3 times.

BO rem 15 (15, 15, 15, 17, 19, 19) sts.

Assembly and Finishing

Block all pieces to size.

Sew the front to back at shoulders.

Collar

With the right side of knitting facing you, pick up and knit 3 sts from the right back neck edge, 22 (24, 26, 28, 30, 32, 32) sts from the back st holder, 3 sts from the left back neck edge, 21 sts from left front neck edge, 16 (18, 20, 22, 24, 26, 26) sts from the front st holder, and 21 sts from right front neck edge 86 (90, 94, 98, 102, 106, 106) sts.

Knitting in the round, k one round decreasing 3 sts evenly spaced along the back edge, and decrease 6 sts evenly spaced along the front edge. K one round without decreases. Reverse direction so you are working from the wrong side of the sweater and BO loosely. Steam block opening so it lies flat.

Sleeves and Side seams:

Center the sleeves over the shoulder seams and sew to the sides of the front and back. Sew the sleeve and front and back side seams tog.

Progressive Color Yarn Variation

What a difference a change in yarn color can make! This piece is knit with the same basic set-in sleeve pattern except I used yarn which changes colors gradually throughout the skein of yarn. You can use one color group, which will create a repeating stripe, or change color groups throughout the piece as I did in the sample project so the finished sweater only repeats the same colors once or twice. This technique takes extra yarn and planning so that you line up the colors for each section of the sweater, but it creates an interesting color change rather than a repeating stripe.

Skill level

INTERMEDIATE

Yarn used for sample shown

Knit One Crochet Too's Paint Box (100% wool, 1.75 oz., 100 yd.), 4 balls in #04 Borealis (color A), 6 balls in #11 Nordic Sky (color B), and 2 balls in #19 Petunia (color C).

Work all pieces the same as the Basic Set-in Sleeve Sweater using the variegated skeins to achieve the color changes. You will need to begin each section at the same color section of the skein, which might mean finding where the first color you want to use begins on the skein and breaking the yarn there on each ball so each section begins with the same color. Also, make sure that you have the yarn in the same color direction so that if, for instance, the color sequence is blue-green-gray, that you don't start one section in the wrong order, or you might have a sleeve that is different in progression than the rest of the sweater.

The key to keeping the gradual color change is to attach each new ball of yarn so that it continues the same color as the old ball for a little bit. Begin the back, front and sleeves with A, then use two balls of B for the back and the front and one ball for each sleeve. End with as many balls of C as needed to complete each piece. You will need more for the larger sizes. (The sample was made to fit a 38" bust.) You will need to find the colors that match or most closely match from one ball to another, and attach the new ball of yarn at this section of the color sequence.

On the sample I made, the blue-gray section of each ball closely match from one ball to the next, so that is where I attached the balls. I found it easiest to wind a large ball using the balls of yarn in the sequence I wanted for each section of the sweater before beginning. So before I began the back, I broke the first ball of A so that it began at the purple section, then wound it until I was at the last blue-gray section, then found the blue-gray section of B and tied those ends together. Then I continued winding with B, attaching another ball of B, and making sure that the colors attached at the same color on the ball and were in the same order.

Finally, I attached C in the same manner, so I ended up with a large ball, enough to knit the whole back of the sweater. I repeated this for the front and each sleeve, except that the sleeve only needed colors A and B to complete them. The balls gradually changed color through the three different color schemes of the yarn. It was a bit of work at the beginning, but then I could just knit the sweater without working a color pattern.

Sampler Textured Variation

This variation on the Basic Set-In Sleeve Sweater uses a sampling of patterns from stitch pattern sections throughout the book, placing them not only down the center front of the sweater, but also along the cuffs of the sleeves, and the center back for added detailing. You can also use this pattern for the dropped shoulder sweater if you prefer to concentrate on the patterns with less work on the shaping details.

Overall Dotted Pattern Chart

Skill level

EXPERIENCED

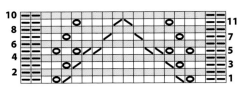

Back Pattern Chart

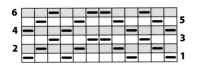

Sleeve Mountain Pattern Chart

Front Sampler Pattern Chart (pattern is continued on next page)

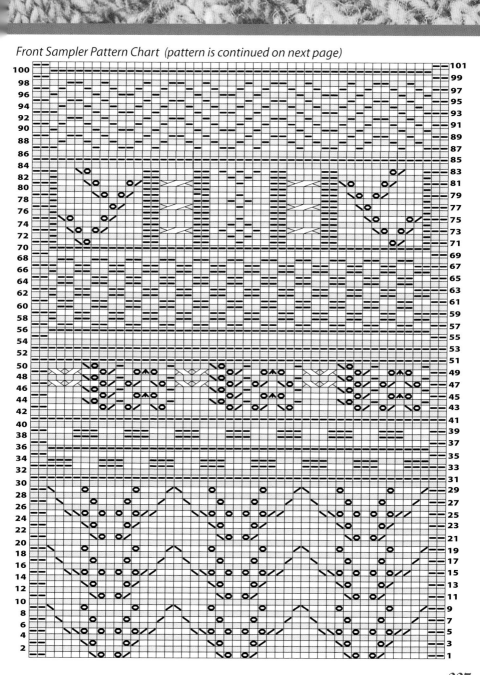

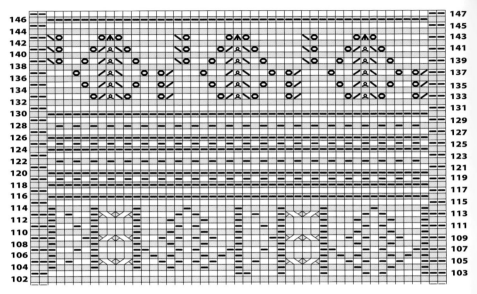

Use the same gauge yarn and needles as the Basic Set-In Sleeve Sweater and follow all shaping details throughout the pieces. CO for the back and knit two rows. Beg with row 3, use stitch markers to separate the center 20 sts, and work the Back patt chart for these sts, and the Overall Dotted patt for the remaining sts. For the front, CO and knit two rows. Beg with row 3, use stitch markers to separate the center 49 sts, and work the Front Sampler patt chart for these sts and the Overall Dotted patt for the remaining sts. After working the chart, work any remaining rows of the center 49 sts in pattern #6 Moss Stitch (page 80). For the sleeves, work the first 14 rows in the Sleeve Mountain patt chart and the remainder of the sleeves in the Overall Dotted patt. Assemble and finish as for the Basic Set-In Sleeve Sweater.

Socks

Socks are great little learning projects. They don't take a huge amount of time or investment of yarn, yet you have the opportunity to practice working with double pointed needles (or two circulars), and you get to decrease and pick up stitches in odd places, miraculously creating a turned heel that fits a person's foot so nicely. Until you actually make a sock they can seem a bit daunting with all these details, but if you try a few you might find out why they become so addicting to many knitters. The one trick that seems to solve the "I never made the second part of the pair" issue, is to either have two sets of needles and work each section of the socks at the same time, or to start the next sock as soon as you finish the first, before you set it aside to begin a different project.

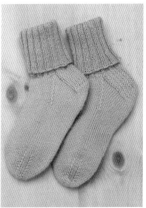
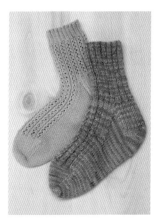

Basic Socks

Following are basic instructions for an average sized woman's sock (shoe size 6 to 9), using DK weight yarn or a sock weight yarn. In the samples shown, the blue calf length sock was made using the DK weight yarn, and the striped ankle length sock was made using a sock weight yarn. If you are new to sock knitting, it will be easier to use the DK weight yarn, since there are less stitches and the yarn and needles are larger. You can easily customize these patterns with decorative stitches throughout this book as shown on the pages following this pattern.

Skill level

INTERMEDIATE

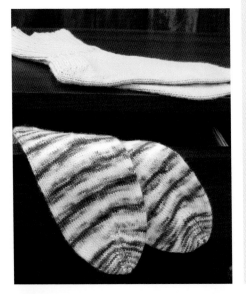

Finished Size
To fit size women's size 6–9 foot

SUPER FINE   LIGHT

Materials

Two 50 g balls of DK weight (sock weight) yarn

Size 6 (Size 3 dpn for cast on)

Size 3 (Size 1) dpn

Tapestry needle

Stitch markers

Gauge

Using smaller needles and yarn in stockinette stitch
26 (36) sts and 32 (46) rows = 4"

Yarn used for samples shown

DK weight socks: Jaeger Matchmaker Merino Double Knitting (100% pure wool, 1.75 oz., 131 yd.) three balls in shade 864 Feather.

Sock weight socks: The Purled Llama Yarn Co.'s Dulce (100% superwash merino wool, 3.5 oz., 440 yd.) in color Caramel Apple.

Cuff and leg

Using the larger needles CO 56 (72) sts, join into a circle, pm. Change to the smaller needles and work in k2, p2 rib for 7" for a calf length sock, or 2½" for an ankle length sock. Remove st marker.

Optional: to place "seam" at center back of sock, k14 (18) sts before beginning the heel section.

Heel

Working back and forth on two needles over 28 (36) sts, work as foll:

Row 1: Working from the inside of the sock, purl across all 28 (36) sts.

Row 2: (Sl 1, k1), repeat across.

Row 3: Sl 1 purlwise, purl remaining sts.

Repeat row 2 and 3 a total of 15 (17) times. You will have 15 (17) slipped st rows, which are the longer sts, and 30 (34) rows total, and the heel will be about 2¼" long.

Turning the Heel

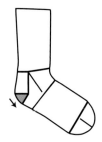

Shape heel as foll for DK weight socks:
Row 1: K16, SKP, k1, turn - 9 sts on left needle before turning, 27 sts total.
Row 2: Sl 1, p5, p2tog, p1, turn - 9 sts on left needle before turning, 26 sts total.
Row 3: Sl 1, k6, SKP, k1, turn - 7 sts on left needle before turning, 25 sts total.
Row 4: Sl 1, p7, p2tog, p1, turn - 7 sts on left needle before turning, 24 sts total.
Row 5: Sl 1, k8, SKP, k1, turn - 5 sts on left needle before turning, 23 sts total.
Row 6: Sl 1, p9, p2tog, p1, turn - 5 sts on left needle before turning, 22 sts total.
Row 7: Sl 1, k10, SKP, k1, turn - 3 sts on left needle before turning, 21 sts total.
Row 8: Sl 1, p11, p2tog, p1, turn - 3 sts on left needle before turning, 20 sts total.

Row 9: Sl 1, k12, SKP, k1, turn - 1 sts on left needle before turning, 19 sts total.
Row 10: Sl 1, p13, p2tog, p2, turn - 0 sts on left needle before turning, 18 sts total.

Shape heel as foll for sock weight socks:
Row 1: K22, SKP, k1, turn - 11 sts on left needle before turning, 35 sts total.
Row 2: Sl 1, p9, p2tog, p1, turn - 11 sts on left needle before turning, 34 sts total.
Row 3: Sl 1, k10, SKP, k1, turn - 9 sts on left needle before turning, 33 sts total.
Row 4: Sl 1, p11, p2tog, p1, turn - 9 sts on left needle before turning, 32 sts total.
Row 5: Sl 1, k12, SKP, k1, turn - 7 sts on left needle before turning, 31 sts total.
Row 6: Sl 1, p13, p2tog, p1, turn - 7 sts on left needle before turning, 30 sts total.
Row 7: Sl 1, k14, SKP, k1, turn - 5 sts on left needle before turning, 29 sts total.
Row 8: Sl 1, p15, p2tog, p1, turn - 5 sts on left needle before turning, 28 sts total.
Row 9: Sl 1, k16, SKP, k1, turn - 3 sts on left needle before turning, 27 sts total.
Row 10: Sl 1, p17, p2tog, p1, turn - 3 sts on left needle before turning, 26 sts total.
Row 11: Sl 1, k18, SKP, k1, turn - 1 sts on left needle before turning, 25 sts total.
Row 12: Sl 1, p19, p2tog, p2, turn - 0 sts on left needle before turning, 24 sts total.

Gusset and Instep

Working in the round on all stitches and needles, arrange the stitches on the needles as foll:
K across 9 (12) heel sts to center of back of heel. Using a new needle (needle #1), knit the remaining 9 (12) heel sts. Continuing with needle #1, pick up and knit 15 (18) sts along left side of heel. With a new needle (needle #2), knit all 28 (36) sts from cuff section not worked for heel. With the last needle (needle #3), pick up and knit 15 (18) sts along remaining side of heel and the 9 (12) remaining heel stitches - 76 (96) sts. 28 (36) sts on needle #2, 24 (30) sts on needles #1 and #3.
Needle #1: Knit to the last 3 sts on the needle, k2tog, k 1.
Needle #2: Knit all sts.
Needle #3: K1, SKP, k remaining sts on needle.
Work one round without decreases.
Repeat these two rounds 12 times - 52 (72) sts total.

Foot

Work even in St st for 5" or until 2" less than desired length of foot, measured from heel to toe.

Toe

Place markers dividing 26 (36) stitches for the top of the sock and the 26 (36) stitches for the bottom of the sock. Work the remaining rounds as foll: after the first marker, k1, k2tog, k to 3 sts from next marker, SKP, k1. Repeat between next marker. Knit one round without decreases. Repeat these two rounds until 20 sts remain. On the next round *k2tog, k to 2 sts from the next marker, SKP. Rep from *. Graft front and back sts tog. Weave in ends.
Lace patt repeat
Row 1: (P1, k4, p1) repeat across.
Row 2: (P1, k2, yo, SKP, p1) repeat across.
Row 3: Repeat row 1.
Row 4: (P1, k2tog, yo, k2, p1) repeat across.

Lace Sock Variation

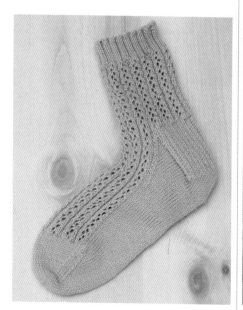

Cable Sock Variation

Using the needles and yarn for the DK weight yarn, CO 56 sts, work the cable patt below for 5", or until desired length to ankle. Work remaining part of sock as basic DK weight instructions, continuing the cable pattern on the top 30 sts until the toe. Work the toe as the basic DK weight instructions.

Cable patt repeat
Row 1–3: (K2, p2) repeat around.
Row 4: (K2, p2, RC1x1, p2) repeat around.

Skill level

INTERMEDIATE

Using the needles and yarn for the sock weight yarn, CO and work a k2, p2 rib patt for 1½". Change to lace patt below for 4". Work remaining part of sock as basic sock weight instructions, continuing the lace pattern on the top 28 sts on needle #2 until the toe. Work the toe as the basic DK weight instructions.

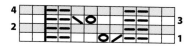

Gloves

Like socks, gloves can be a bit daunting before you make your first pair. They look difficult, with all the small finger sections worked on double pointed needles. But, like socks, once you make a pair of gloves, you see how little there is to it, just the cuff, the hand and all the finger sections. The fingers are actually so small and are basically the same process over and over again, that once you know gloves, they aren't so complex after all. One thing nice about gloves is that each glove takes less time to make than the arm of a sleeve on a sweater, and once you get used to them, they are wonderful items to showcase your knitting skills or try out new stitches and patterns while making a useful and special gift. This pattern is for gloves using worsted or sock weight yarn to fit an average sized hand.

Basic Gloves

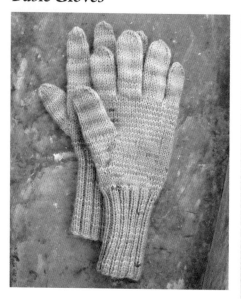

Skill level

INTERMEDIATE

Notes:
To increase for gusset, knit into the back of the strand between the stitches.

To add 1 stitch between fingers, knit into the front and the back of the last stitch before joining the palm side to the back side at the base of the finger.

To add 2 stitches between fingers, knit into the front, the back, and the front of the last stitch before joining the palm side to the back side at the base of the finger.

Finished Size
To fit medium women's hand 4" across palm

Materials
Two 1.75 oz. skein worsted sock weight yarn

One set Size 4 (size 3) 6" dpn

Tapestry needle

Embroidery thread

Sock weight Gloves: Koigu KPM (100% merino wool, 1.75 oz., 175 yd.), 2 skeins in #2097.

Worsted weight Gloves: The Purled Llama Yarn Co.'s Carino (50% superfine alpaca/50% wool, 4 oz., 500 yd.) in color Wisdom.

Gauge
Gauge in stockinette stitch using the smaller needles and yarn 28 sts and 36 rows = 4"

Yarn used for samples shown
Sock weight gloves: Koigu KPM (100% merino wool, 1.75 oz., 175 yd), 2 skeins in #2097.

Worsted weight gloves: The Purled Llama Yarn Co.'s Carino (50% superfine alpaca/50% wool, 4 oz., 500 yd) in color Wisdom.

Left Glove
Cuff and Body

CO 44 (48) sts, join into a circle, placing marker at the beg of the round.

Work 2k, p2 rib for 4".

Cont knitting in the round in St st for 6 rounds.

On the next round, inc 1 st on both sides of the first st in the round.

K 2 rounds even in St st.

On the next round, inc 1 st at the beg of the round, k3, inc 1, knit around.

K 2 rounds even in St st.

On the next round, inc 1 st at the beg of the round, k5, inc 1, knit around.

Rep the 3 round patt 2 more times, knitting 7, then 9 sts between increases at the beg of the inc rounds - 54 (58) sts.

Use provisional cast on to CO 8 sts at beg of round, move 11 thumb sts to scrap of yarn, knit around - 51 (55) sts on needles.

K 3 sts, k2tog, continue in St st around - 50 (54) sts.

Work around in St st.

K3 sts, k2tog, continue in St st around - 49 (53) sts.

Work around in St st.

K3, k2tog, continue in St st around - 48 (52) sts.

Work even in St st for 8 (10) more rounds, ending the last round 1 st before the stitch marker, remove the stitch marker.

Pointer finger

Continuing with the yarn from the Cuff and Body, pick up the next 13 sts over 3 needles, casting on 2 more sts by knitting into the front, the back and the front of the 13th st. Move the remaining stitches to a scrap of yarn - 16 sts for pointer finger.

Work even in the round until the pointer finger is 2¼" long, or ¼" from the top of the finger.

Fold the knitting so it lays flat between the palm and the back and mark the sides.

On the next round make a centered double decrease at each side - 12 sts.

Work the next round even.

On the next round make a centered double decrease at each side again - 8 sts.

Cut the yarn to 8" and pass through all the remaining sts.

Weave in end.

Thumb

Pick up the 11 sts from the thumb gusset, 1 (2) sts on ea side, and 8 sts from the CO section of the thumb hole - 21 (23) sts.

Rnd 1: Knit.

Rnd 2: Dec 1 st at the center of the 8 CO sts of the thumb hole - 20 (22) sts.

Rnd 3: Knit.

Rnd 4: Dec 1 st above the previous dec - 19 (21) sts.

Rnd 5–8: Rep rnd 3 and rnd 4 - 18 (20) then 17 (19) sts.

Work even until ¼" from top of thumb.

Fold the thumb so it lays flat as shown at right and mark the sides.

On the next round make a centered double decrease at each side of thumb - 13 (15) sts.

Work the next round even.

On the next round make a centered double decrease at each side again - 9 (11) sts.

Cut the yarn to 8" and pass through all the remaining sts.

Weave in end.

Middle finger

Pick up 6 from the front, CO 2 sts between front and back, pick up 6 from the back, and pick up 2 more sts from the finished finger - 16 sts.

Work even until 2½" long, or ¼" from the top of the finger.

Fold the finger so it lays flat and mark the sides.

On the next round make a centered double decrease at each side - 12 sts.

Work the next round even.

On the next round make a centered double decrease at each side again - 8 sts.

Cut the yarn to 8" and pass through all the remaining sts.

Weave in end.

Ring finger

Work the same as the Middle Finger.

Little finger

Pick up the remaining 11 (14) sts for the little finger, pick up 2 more stitch between fingers - 13 (16) sts.

K 3 rounds.

On the next round, dec 1 st above the 2 sts between fingers - 12 (15) sts.

Work 3 rounds even, then dec 1 st in the same place as before - 11 (14) sts.

Work even until 1¾" long, or ¼" from the top of the finger.

Fold the finger so it lays flat and mark the sides.

On the next round make a centered double decrease at each side - 7 (10) sts.

Work the next round even.

On the next round make a centered double decrease at each side again - 3 (6) sts.

Cut the yarn to 8" and pass through all the remaining sts.

Weave in end. Block gloves to size.

Making it your size

To adjust the pattern for larger or smaller sizes, measure snuggly around the palm of the hand and multiply that number by the number of stitches per inch of your yarn. This will be the number of stitches to cast on. Follow the instructions for the Cuff and Body, trying on the knitting as you get to each section to make sure it will fit. For the fingers, I like to thread the stitches onto small (about 6") lengths of yarn, one for each finger, then I tie each one into a circle and try the glove on to see if the fingers will be the right size. This is a good method, when you are not sure how many stitches you will need for each finger, because you can try it several times until you get the correct grouping of stitches. Once you have determined how many stitches you want in each finger, it's a simple matter of knitting one finger at a time from each group, adding two stitches between fingers.

Glossary

Afghan weight

A thick weight yarn, usually about 4 stitches to the inch, commonly used for making small blankets, called afghans. Number 4, "Medium" in the Standard Yarn Weight System guide.

Appliqué

A decorative design attached to the surface of a project usually by stitching the perimeter of the design to the base material.

Aran

A highly textured style of design characterized by multiple combinations of high relief patterns worked in columns with a large central pattern, bordered by smaller patterns on either side.

Aran weight

A thick yarn, usually about 4 stitches to the inch, commonly used for making Aran-style designs. Number 4, Medium in the Standard Yarn Weight System guide.

Back stitch

A decorative embroidery stitch and a firm structural stitch made by working small adjacent stitches on the front of the piece and long overlapping stitches on the back. This stitch is often used to outline design elements in embroidery, and to attach shoulder seams in knitting.

Bind off

Ending a piece of knitting by locking all the live stitches together so they won't unravel.

Block

The process of dampening finished knitting, shaping it to the desired finished size and letting it dry.

Bulky weight

A very thick weight of yarn, generally less than 3 stitches to the inch. Number 6, "Super Bulky" in the Standard Yarn Weight System guide.

Cable needle

A short double pointed needle that is used to hold unused stitches in front of or in back of the working stitches for making cable designs.

Cable

A pattern element characterized by one or more stitches that have been worked out of order so that the resulting pattern has a twist in the columns of stitches.

Cast on

Making and placing the beginning stitches on a knitting needle.

Chunky weight
An extra thick weight yarn, generally less than 4 stitches to the inch. Number 5, "Bulky" in the Standard Yarn Weight System guide.

Circular Needle
Knitting needles that have points at both ends with a central section of flexible cord.

DK weight
A medium/light weight yarn, generally about 5 to 7 stitches to the inch, used for double knitting (DK). Number 3, "Light" in the Standard Yarn Weight System guide.

Decrease
To change the number of stitches on the needle to a lower number of stitches, by several methods such as knitting two stitches together as one, so there are less stitches on the needle for the next row.

Double Knitting
A medium/light weight yarn, generally about 5 to 7 stitches to the inch, commonly called DK weight yarn. Number 3, "Light" in the Standard Yarn Weight System guide.

Double-pointed Needle
Straight needles that are pointed at both ends. Sold in sets of 4 or 5 needles.

Duplicate Stitch
Also known as Swiss Darning, a decorative embroidery stitch made by following the yarn path of stockinette stitch to add a different color to the finished knitting.

Dye Lot Number
A unique number assigned to all skeins of yarn dyed at the same time. When purchasing yarn, choosing all skeins of a color with the same dye lot number ensures the colors will all be exactly the same.

Ease
Stretching or slightly gathering an edge to fit in place. Used mostly when seaming sleeves in place to the front and the back of finished sweaters.

Eyelet
A decorative hole made in knitting by working a yarn over (yo) on one row, then working the strand made by the yarn over as if it is a stitch in the next row.

Fair Isle
A colorwork technique and style of knitting, in which decorative color patterns are worked in stockinette stitch by using two colors of yarn in each row.

Fingering weight

A thin weight yarn, generally 7 to 9 sts to the inch, used to make socks, lace and baby items. Number 1, "Super Fine" in the Standard Yarn Weight System guide.

Gauge

The number of stitches per inch and rows per inch on a knitted project, usually measured over 4".

Hank

A wound length of yarn.

Increasing

Adding more stitches to the needle, made in a number of different techniques including making yarn overs, adding stitches at the end of a row, knitting into the back and the front of the same stitch, or knitting in the strand of yarn between stitches.

Intarsia

A colorwork technique in which sections of color which are grouped over several stitches and rows are worked without stranding, and the yarn is twisted at the edge of the color on the back of the work, dropped for the remainder of the row, then picked up and worked again when reached on the next row.

Knitwise

Inserting the needle into a stitch as if to knit, which is into the front of the stitch, from the right side of the stitch to the left side of the stitch.

Lace weight

A very fine yarn, usually 10 or more stitches to the inch. Not listed on the Standard Yarn Weight System guide, but it is usually grouped with Number 1 "Super Fine" since that is the closest group.

Light worsted weight

A medium weight yarn, usually about 4 sts to the inch, used mostly in the United States. Number 3, "Light" in the Standard Yarn Weight System guide.

Live stitches

Stitches in progress in knitting, which can unravel when not on the needle or a stitch holder

Mattress stitch

A sewing stitch used to seam finished knitted pieces together, by taking a small stitch on one edge of the piece, then taking a small stitch on the edge of the other piece and pulling the stitches snuggly to draw the edges together.

Needle Gauge
A flat device with different sized holes to insert knitting needles or crochet hooks to measure the size of the tool.

Pattern repeat
A single section of a pattern that is then worked the number of times desired to make the pattern continue over the row of knitting.

Point protector
A cover for the end of knitting needles to protect the working stitches from sliding off the needle and to keep the point of the needle from damaging surrounding items.

Purlwise
Inserting the needle into a stitch as if to purl, which is into the front of the stitch, from the left side of the stitch to the right side of the stitch.

Ribbing
A knitting pattern traditionally made of knit/purl patterned vertical stripes, used at the waist, cuffs and neck of a sweater, which pulls in more than the rest of the knitting, and has more stretch.

Selvedge stitch
A stitch worked at the edge of a piece in addition to any pattern instructions, used as an added section where the finished pieces will be sewn together.

Slub
Along a length of yarn, a thick section or imperfection that creates a bump in the yarn.

Sock weight
A thin yarn, usually 7 or more stitches to the inch, used for knitting socks. Number 2, "Fine" in the Standard Yarn Weight System guide.

Sport weight
A light weight yarn, usually 5 to 6 stitches to the inch, used for making light weight garments and baby items. Number 2, "Fine" in the Standard Yarn Weight System guide.

Steam blocking
Using a steam iron to dampen finished knitting before shaping it to the finished size. The iron is held above the knitting, never pressed on the surface of the knitting.

Stitch Holder

A small needle with some type of cap or closure so you can slide stitches onto it and keep them in place while working a different section of the piece. Then you go back and move the stitches from the stitch holder back to the working needle and continue knitting.

Stitch Marker

A small ring to slide onto the knitting needle to mark a pattern detail, such as a place to increase or decrease, or a color or pattern change. When you get to the stitch marker on the row, you slide it from the left needle to the right needle, and continue knitting.

Stranding

In colorwork, stranding is when you hold the color not in use to the backside of the work until needed. The result is long and short strands of yarn across each row on the back side of the finished knitting.

Swiss darning

Another term for duplicate stitch.

Tapestry needle

A large blunt ended needle, large enough to thread with yarn.

Worsted weight

An all purpose medium weight yarn, usually about 4 stitches to the inch, used for making a variety of items including sweaters and blankets. Number 4, Medium in the Standard Yarn Weight System guide.

Yarn weights

Generally, the thickness of yarn.

Index

Supply Sources

Yarn from the following companies was used for the projects in this book. All the swatches except for the color work section were knit using Louet's Gems superwash 100% merino wool yarn in sport weight. Look for these and other yarns at your favorite yarn store.

Brown Sheep Co.
www.brownsheep.com

Lion Brand
www.lionbrand.com

Lorna's Laces
www.lornaslaces.net

Louet
www.louet.com

Mountain Colors
www.mountaincolors.com

Koigu
www.koigu.com

Kureon by Noro
www.knittingfever.com

Rowan Yarns
www.westminsterfibers.com
www.knitrowan.com

The Purled Llama
www.thepurledllama.com

About the Author

Jane Davis is a highly sought-after instructor for knitting and beadwork. She is a regular contributing editor for Classic Elite Yarn Company and the author of several books, including *Bead Embroidery: The Complete Guide*, *Felted Crochet* and *The Complete Guide to Beading Techniques*.

Knit and Crochet Your Way to Great Gifts

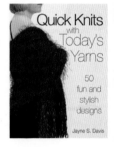